T0116806

He is coming Soon

A look at our world today

By

Dell Watson

Trafford rev. 07/25/2011

 www.trafford.com

North America & international
toll-free: 1 888 232 4444 (USA & Canada)
phone: 250 383 6864 ♦ fax: 812 355 4082

CONTENTS

INTRODUCTION

"For God so loved the world that he gave his only begotten son, that whosoever believeth in him should not perish but have everlasting life." (John 3:16). *"But God commendeth his love towards us, in that while we were yet sinners, Christ died for us"* (Romans 5:8). "In this was manifested the love of God toward us, because that God sent his only begotten son into the world, that we might live through him." (1 John 4:9).

I am free, I am free, no longer bound, and I praise God that my soul has been released from sin and shame. Now that Jesus has come and died on the cross for my sins and your sins, we now have a free will to live this life in accordance to the will of God. When Jesus died on the cross we truly became free indeed. That means all people all over the world. Being a black male, I understand freedom well. The freedom Malcolm X, and Dr. King fought for. The freedom Jesus died for released all people from eternal sin, meaning when we die we do not have to die in our sins and spend eternity in hell fire.

When my soul was bound, Jesus death and resurrection lifted me, and for that reason my soul is glad.

Many Christians do not truly understand spiritual freedom and what it means. Because He loved us so much, God carefully planned the sacrifice of his Son to provide for our freedom from his wrath and our growth in his love. This life that we live is all about God, and we as a people should want to fully understand God's purpose for our lives. Without knowing and understanding who God is, what his will is for our life, then we have no hope in this life or for eternity, nor will we understand what spiritual freedom means. Before Jesus died, we were a guilty people not fit for the Kingdom of the Almighty God. This hold that the world has on you is not from God, but the devil! Satan has a strong hold on your life and you are dead spiritually to what is going on around you. Jesus is the one and only person that can remove your burdens His sacrifice freed us by paying the penalty for all sins. By His going to the cross and taking our punishment, we can now have fellowship with God himself, because we have accepted Christ as our Savior.

God's goal for us after we have become one of His children, is freedom from bitterness, hate, malice, and to love others as we love ourselves. Forgiveness should be part of our life. When you have accomplished all this in your life, then and only then can you say you are free from the world and what it has to offer.

CHAPTER ONE

A Rebellious People

We have completely left God out of our daily lives. Doing so has caused us to become a corrupt people. We as adults do not respect one another, just as children do not respect adults. This explains why most children in the world are skeptical about trusting adults. They have good reason not to. I remember when I was a child not only having trust in my parents, but in all adults. Their word was good on any concern.

However, it seems the baby boom population is failing to uphold the same standards. Many times people today have little to no reservation when it comes to lying. The youth in America have little faith in teachers, coaches, preachers, and our government because they are constantly let down. They hear adults say one thing, and yet they see adults doing the opposite. We have fallen from grace and the presence of God. These are the last days that we are living in.

God had become so angry with man in the days of Noah, that He said he repented that he made man. Mankind was wicked on the earth and God saw that the wickedness of man was great and that every thought of his heart was continuously evil, and it repented the Lord that he had made man on the earth, and it grieved him at his heart. God said, *"I will destroy man whom I have created from the face of the earth both man and beast and the creeping thing, and the fowls of the air: for it repenteth me that I have made them."* (Genesis 6: 5-7).

Now, when Jesus walked the earth, his disciples asked him to tell them when the end of time would come. *"As he sat upon the Mount of Olives the disciples came unto him privately saying, tell us when shall these things be? And what shall be the sign of thy coming, and of the end of the world? And Jesus answered and said unto them, Take heed that no man deceive you. For many shall come in my name saying I **am** Christ and shall deceive many. And ye shall hear of wars and rumors of wars.* (Matthew 24:6-51). We have become an evil generation and many of us are not trying to change. Today many children feel they are not loved or wanted by their parents. As a result, many run away from home and become very rebellious toward their parents. God said to fathers, *"Fathers provoke not your children to wrath but bring them up in the nurture and admonition of the Lord."* (Ephesians 5:21-6:4).

One of the biggest problems we face today is, children having children, and being totally unprepared to care for a baby. Many girls become pregnant around the age of 14 and up. They are not only physically immature, but also mentally and emotionally immature. I see trouble all over the world and I see where man has just made a mess on God's earth. Man doesn't have the first correct idea about how to heal the land, but he would have people believe he is on top of everything. How can man be on top of things when God is on the move? We are in the beginning of sorrows and with no hope, but our only hope is in Christ Jesus. Man doesn't have any answers for changing or fixing anything in the world, but when you listen to men speak he would have you to believe he is on top of every problem this world faces. The world needs to go down on their knees and repent to God before the end comes. One should not listen when men say that everything is going to be all right. Unemployment rates are yet rising, prisons are overflowing, hospitals are full, divorce rates are high, young girls are having babies, homelessness is prevalent, poor people are overlooked, crime is towering, drugs have taken over our world, and prayer has been taken out of the schools! In the meantime, we are standing by waiting for politicians to correct these issues. However, they are not able to help themselves. Jesus is our only hope, He is saying, *"Will you come unto me?"* Yet we never give Him a chance. *"Peace, I leave with you, my peace I give unto you not as the world giveth, give I unto you. Let not your heart be troubled, neither let it be afraid."* (John 14:27).

I can remember vividly when the removal of prayer was taken out of the schools. That was the worst thing that could have happened. This made God very angry, and now we are living the results. Children are taking guns to school and shooting classmates. Teachers are afraid of students, drugs are on campuses and it is going to get worse day by day. God is the only one who can change our situations, but He was taken out of the schools. Children are denied from hearing what God had to say to them through The Bible. They are not allowed to take a Bible to school.

There are many men preaching in these last days, but many of them are deceiving people. This is because the Word of God is not being read in our homes daily. We even have women calling themselves preachers. If women knew God, they would know this has never been so, but man is letting her assume the role of being the head of churches. Men are so weak-minded and allow woman to do whatever it is they want to do. God is angry with this.

God never intended for it to be this way, for a woman to call herself a pastor or preacher. When she is a pastor of a church, she is over the man, because the pastor is the head of the church. *"Wives submit yourselves unto your own husbands, as unto the Lord. For the husband is the head of the wife, even as Christ is the head of the church and He is the Savior of the body."* (Ephesians 5:21-33).

This means a woman should not pastor man. This is not the order of God. He does not want her as the head of the man in any capacity. Man being so foolish and weak has sat back and watched women try and take over the world. God Himself will not let this happen. Please do not misunderstand I think women are the most beautiful creatures God could have made. However, just like men, women will have to answer to this right before God. We as people often operate on impulse seeking to gratify ourselves. We fail to consult God concerning our lives. I can remember a time when a woman didn't want to be the head of a man. In this day and age I hear many women saying, "Well the man is too slow, or he is not doing things the way they should be done." This is just an excuse for them to get into a man's roll. *"But suffer not a woman to teach nor to usurp authority over the man, but to be in silence.* (1Timothy 2:12).

I look everyday at man's law, and I have never believed in it, but I obey his laws because it is right before God. Man makes his laws but he does not live by them. He would break them everyday if it is to his or her benefit. It has gotten so bad that if a policeman tries to pull a motorist over, he or she is afraid to stop. You may fear that the officer might inflict violence or you might question whether the officer is legitimate. One may be damned if they do or damned if they don't. This is how it is these days and there are many more like them ahead.

"This know also, that in the last days, perilous times shall come for men shall be lovers of their own selves, covetous, boasters, proud, blasphemous, disobedient to parents, unthankful, unholy, without natural affection, true breakers, false accusers, incontinent, fierce, despisers of those that are good, traitors, heady, high-minded, lovers of pleasures more than lovers of God; Having a form of Godliness, but denying the power thereof: from such turn away." (II Timothy 3:1-5).

Something I have never understood until God revealed it to me, the KKK constantly declared that God didn't love Black people, only Caucasian people. So they burned Black churches, hanged Black men, raped Black women, burned Black people's homes and they said it was all done for the Lord. First of all, they do not know God, nor do they know the Bible. *"If a man says, I love God, and hate his brother, he is a liar: for he that loveth not his brother whom he hath seem, how can he love God whom he hath not seen?"* (I John 4:20-21).

Everywhere you look people have their own churches, every race has its own church, yet we supposedly serve the same God. There is but one heaven and one hell, and with God there is only one race. *"For there is no respecter of person with God."* (Roman 2:11). God loves all people equally.

We as people have heard lies so long that we are beginning to believe them, and live by them. That is one reason our churches are separated and divided into racial groups. When we do this we are not pleasing God, but the devil. I want you to know the devil also has preachers, and many of them are gone out into the world preaching and teaching, but they are false. *"Beloved, believe not every spirit, but try the spirits whether they are of God because many false prophets are gone out into the world."* (I John 4:3). The reason many of us do not know God and His Word (The Bible) is because we don't read it, we'd rather pretend that we know the Word of God. *"Study to show thyself approved unto God, a workman that needed not to be ashamed, rightly dividing the word of truth"* (II Timothy 2:15). We don't have any excuse for not knowing the Word of God. God wishes that everyone would make it to heaven, but man's evilness of heart and not humbling himself before God, and repenting of his sins will cause him to lift his eyes in Hell. I talk to people every day, many of them are totally lost, and they do not want to know Jesus because they love sin more than God. Man loves darkness because his deeds are evil.

Many adults wonder why their children are on drugs and do not respect them. Children have a hard time listening to their parents or any adult these days because they see adults as liars, promise breakers and evildoers. Children tell me all the time many of their parents do drugs with them. Parents are not setting an example, and children are so out of hand today that parents do not know what to do with them, so they let the law handle their children. If parents would train their children like the Bible reads, crime rates would decrease, teen pregnancy would not be so high. Parents have lost their way with their children and God. Fathers and mothers are on drugs, incest continues to increase, children are killing their parents, parents are killing their children, this war goes on and on.

Sinners are losing out with God because of the spirit of rebellion. When I was a little boy, on Sunday mornings about 6:00 am in the morning, everybody in the house had to get up to pray. My grandfather saw to it that this went on until I was old enough to leave home. I would get really mad at having to get up so early for prayer. Now that I am an adult, I thank God for my grandfather.

I want to be a saved man who loves God, a man that fears God, but above all, a man who obeys the laws of God. We are in a very dangerous time. The devil is on the move and many of us are yet in our sins. It looks as if time will catch many people still living sinfully. The days have become full of terror and terrorism. One does not know who can be trusted any more. Man does not fear God, this is why he performs so many evil deeds.

All that surrounds me in this present world is sadness. Sometimes it overwhelms me. I never thought I would see the time when families would start shooting one another, but it is happening. In this world there does not seem to be anyone who wants to help their fellow man, everybody is looking out for number one. People's minds are troubled, they are carnally minded and not spiritual minded.

If you go to a church today and you are a preacher, the pastor of that church might ask you for your papers. It happened to me, but I look over men and see Jesus. In the Church of God in Christ, to pastor a church, you must go before a board to be ordained. I cannot, and would not go before a board to be ordained. In my heart, I know it is not right. I feel no man is worthy to ordain me, nor did man call me to preach. *"Before I formed thee in the belly, I knew thee: and before thou camest forth out of the womb I sanctified thee, and I ordained thee a prophet unto the nations."* (Jeremiah 1:5). *"And he ordained twelve, that he might send them forth to preach."* (Mark 3:14). *"Ye have not chosen me, but I have chosen you, and ordained you, that ye should go and bring forth fruit, and that your fruit should remain: that whatsoever ye shall ask of the Father in my name, he may give it to you."* (John15:16).

So you see, in my Bible, I do not read where man has the power to ordain anyone. Many of these meetings that churches have are nothing more than a money racket, no one is really getting saved. Many people will say they are saved, but yet their lives do not line up with the Word of God. Preachers will not tell people the truth. I am determined to follow God all the way to the end. No bishop or superintendent, can tell me I am not ordained. God Himself ordained me to preach the Gospel. God wants His people to have the best understanding of who He is. He does not want us to make worldly possessions our God. Most people in this world live for the so-called finer things in life and never think about their soul. Man wants us to be less concerned about what is really important in life, and that is Jesus Christ.

We always want the government to take care of our problems and society has become very comfortable putting our trust in the government and not God. People around the world better go back to God, for He is our only hope in these last and evil days. I look at the different races around the world, and the Bible never speaks to races, but Jews and Gentiles are His people. If you become a Christian then that makes you one of His people. Man came up with the word races, not God. Man has had us fighting one another for generations. Caucasians don't like Blacks, Blacks don't like Caucasians on and on it goes. God doesn't say things like nigger, redneck or wetback, God loves all people the same. Man started all these prejudicial words, not God. God is love, man is full of evilness and he uses it everyday on people for his gain. Man is ignorant without God in His life, he will do and say whatever the devil leads him to do. We as people should no longer get wrapped up in man's ignorance, but do the will of God. Through his Son Jesus Christ our Lord, for this is who will save us from our sins in the last days. O children of the most high God, do not let man keep deceiving you, turn to God for this is the way. If you would just say, "Lord help me," and really mean it, God will draw near to you. You don't have to be rich, famous, or have good credit. He loves drug dealers, the drug user, He loves prostitutes, He just hates what they do. *"Ye are of God little children, and have overcome them: because greater is he that is in you than he that is in the world"* (I John 4:4). *"What shall we then say to these things? If God be for us who can be against us?"* (Roman 8:31).

God wishes men and women would come to repentance, but Satan has caused many men and women to turn their faces from God. We have come to live in a world of sin and many love it and don't want to change. Sin has overtaken us and many are not troubled by it. This is why we do not have respect for our children, one another, and ourselves. We have begun to justify everything that is wrong. We don't care about what is right. This comes from not serving God, because many of us serve the devil. We need Jesus Christ, for He is the only way. If we don't turn back to Jesus, all the killing, lying, cheating, backstabbing will never stop. We hurt one another at any cost just to get whatever it is we are after. Without

God in our lives, we really have no hope. I am not talking about earthly, but spiritually. God does not care about the things of this world, but he care about every soul. He would love for everyone to be saved from the things of this world because silver and gold will not matter to Him in that day. People of this world are looking up to our presidents, kings, prime ministers, anybody but God. This is sad. These people we look up to are not even in control. Only God is in control of every situation of the world. We are a stubborn people, we do not obey God's laws, we have broken all Ten Commandments. We break them over and over again, we are so rebellious. *"For my people are foolish, they have not known me; they are Sottish children, and they have none understanding: they are wise to do evil, but to do good they have no knowledge."* (Jeremiah 4:22).

The reason we have no knowledge of God is because we'd rather do wrong than right. We like to do evil. Because of our corrupt ways, many people will lift their eyes in hell. God has a judgment against all wickedness. Cruelty has overtaken so many people that we do not even know what love is. Many women and men have no shame about their indecent, heartless and risky behavior. God is very unhappy with the way we are living, and we are not trying to do any better with our lives. The reason we cannot love one another is because we do not have the love giver in our hearts. This is why we cannot forgive each other because there is no God in our hearts. In these last days, we need more and more of God Almighty in our lives. Jesus has all the answers, but Jesus is not who we would like in our lives because we do not want to live according to His will. We are so rebellious and unwise that we think we have all the answers to our world's problems. We are experiencing things we were forewarned about a long time ago.

And Jesus said unto them, "*See ye not all these things? Verily I say unto you, there shall not be left here one stone upon another, that shall not be thrown down.*" (Matt 24:2-13).

The Bible is being fulfilled by the Word of God. This is why I do not believe in the word racism. I call it pure hate when we are just like the scribes and Pharisees, rebellious hypocrites! Everything that is happening in the world today, God Himself has allowed because we are an evil people. "*And I will punish the world for their evil, and the wicked for their iniquity; and I will cause the arrogancy of the proud to cease, and will lay low the haughtiness of the terrible.*" (Isaiah 13;11).

We have lost our way with God, and many people do not want to find God while they have the opportunity. I can remember a time when people trusted law enforcement, but over the years many people of all colors have had some kind of trouble with the law. We have trouble in schools with students, also parents, preachers, and doctors. We look for so many ways to solve our conditions and everything we try on our own does not work.

We cannot fix gun control, so the NRA gets mad at the President for not fixing the problem. Kids are still getting their hands on guns at will. Guns have become this country's number one problem, along with drunk driving. It will never be fixed by man. All the problems that we have in this world are a result of doing things man's way. The thing that is sad is that people are waiting on him to do something about it. However, God is in control of this world. "*If my people, which are called by my name, shall humble themselves, and pray, seek my face, and turn from their wicked ways; then will I hear from heaven, and will forgive their sin, and will heal their land.*" (II Chronicles 7:14). Amen!

CHAPTER TWO

Children & Parents - Who's the Boss?

We have come to a point in this present world, where there is a dilemma between parents and children. In the judgment, parents will answer to God for not raising their children according to His Word. Many times the courts do not hold the parents accountable for their children's actions, but God does. We live in a society that allows the State to raise children whom God gave to parents. Some parents do not want the responsibility of raising their children. Some parents around this country are abusing and even killing their children. Man has created a law called "child abuse," so parents who are trying to bring their children up in the right way, are now afraid to spank their children when they do something wrong.

The police are between a rock and a hard place, so are parents who will not spank their children. Children know there is no punishment by their parents for their wrong, nor by the schools. So many kids do what they want. Many parents do not take their children to Sunday School, or to Sunday morning church services.

Some parents get upset with their kids for drinking, but the parent may be found drinking in front of their children. In many homes there is no structure, nothing to build on but the wrong they see adults do. Most adults tell lies, and many of them lie to children. The children see this and have no respect for the adult.

I am not going to worry about man's law, but I am going to do what God told me and has told every adult. *"Foolishness is bound in the heart of a child; but the rod of correction shall drive it far from him."* (Proverbs 22:15) *"Withhold not correction from the child: for if thou beateth him with the rod, he shall not die. Thou shalt beat him with the rod, and shalt deliver his soul from hell."* (Proverb 23:14) *"Train up a child in the way he should go: and when he is old, he will not depart from it."* (Proverbs 22:6). *"Behold, the third time I am ready to come to you; and I will not be burdensome to you: for I seek not yours, but you: for the children ought not to lay up for the parents, but the parents for children."* (II Corinthians 12:14). *"Children, obey your parents in the Lord: for this is right."* (Ephesians 6:1). *"And ye fathers, provoke not your children to wrath: but bring them up in the nurture and admonition of the Lord."* (Ephesians 6:4). *"He that spareth his rod hateth his son: but he that loveth him chasteneth him betimes."* (Proverbs 13: 24).

Many homes do not have rules for their children to follow, which will help them in life. Many children are raising themselves, or the grandparents are raising them. We have so many parents that are on drugs these days, and some let their kids take drugs with them. Many crack babies do not even have a chance because their mothers shoot up while she is pregnant, so the baby comes into this world addicted to drugs. Also in the school system, teachers want to put kids on a drug called Ritalin to keep kids calm when they are misbehaving or being. I can remember in my day, when you acted up in class, the teacher got the belt out, and then they would send a note home with the kid and he or she would be disciplined all over again. We did not die from getting spanked! When punishment by spanking was taken out of the schools, adults gave children the license to take control of the schools, teachers, parents, and anybody else that might get in their way. And God himself has allowed this because we are disobedient people full of evil. When integration came about, Caucasian parents did not want black teachers spanking their kids, also black parents did not want Caucasian teachers spanking their kids.

The last two years in my public school years I went to a mixed school, and during that time a Caucasian principal spanked me and I did not die. I have never in my life heard the word integrity, honesty, sincerity used by so many people that did not live by those words. Children know adults of today do not live by those words either. Many adults today are lusted and have lusted their children also. I want to serve notice to all the parents around the world; you will stand before God because of all your misdeeds. To you parents that do not raise your children according to God's will have much heartache over the years. *"The fear of the Lord is the beginning of knowledge: but fools despise wisdom and instruction."* (Proverbs 1:7) *"Trust in the Lord with all thane heart; and lean not unto thine own understanding. In all thy ways acknowledge him, and he shall direct thy paths."* (Proverbs 3:5-6)

You see we cannot even begin to formulate ways to change problems in the world. Only God can give us true effective solutions through Jesus Christ. The President of the United States, FBI, CIA, or anybody else cannot out do God. Many children of today are taking care of themselves with no hope. God has given charge to the parents and not the government to raise their children. I look around this world, children have taken a charge of their own lives at a very young age. Smoking, drinking, and staying up all night and many other things that they do. This is a very sin sick world. We have parents who are afraid of their own children. You have some parents who sleep with the door to their bedroom locked each night because they fear their own children. Parents need to turn to God while they can. Men need to take charge and be the head as God planned it. Children need to be in Sunday school every Sunday learning about God. God loves all people, but He does not love the sin in their lives. We as men have been given a job to do by God! We are the head of the house and prayer should be upon every man's lips so that his home can be a praying home. The home will never function properly without God in control. He is our faith, hope, love, joy, peace, and without Him all men will fail. Let no man deceive and tell you there is no God, or that God has no judgement. God is alive and He is waiting for men all over the world to say yes to His will and way. All our sins have come before His face and He is angry. But I will say to the world, try God, He will not fell you. Men that sit in these high positions have been letting you down.

Sometime you feel like you cannot make it, and God is saying to you, *"Will you come, I am He that was dead but I am alive forever more."* God does not need your money, what He wants out of us is to be saved, and living holy, so that your soul will not be lost.

Parents clean your life up now, while God can be found. I want every parent on drugs, who thinks there is no hope, to know God loves you and He will forgive any sin. Some of you all look to man to help you when you become an addict, and many times treatments doesn't help. Jesus is the answer and He will heal you. It has been my experience that children live in fear of today's adults. I hear all the time we have a children problem in today's world, but I strongly disagree. I believe we have an adult problem in this world. Basically, many adults have not grown up! They still want to do the same things kids do. Children are often confused where are my parents? Parents tell their children do not do as I do, even if it is wrong. So when children see their parents drinking, taking drugs, having sex in front of them, they see it as being okay, no matter what their parents tell them. If Mom and Dad do it then it cannot be that bad. In the old days when parents spoke children listened. When adults told you do something, they only told you once. They took their children to Sunday School, not one Sunday, but every Sunday. They showed respect in front of their children, so as children we feared our parents, but at the same time we knew they loved us and we loved them. There was no confusion between the children and parents.

I believe our government made a huge mistake by allowing gay couples to raise children. This is a very bad message for children, a child should not have to come up in that kind of environment. God has never ordained same sex marriages. But God will have the last say on all wrong deeds. Children have a hard road to ride down and it will not get any better for them except for God to help them. Sunday School is more important than public school! If children are not being taken to church to learn about God and His ways, there is no hope for that child or that household. It is sad that many of our foster homes and many State homes are filled with children. Where are the parents that made these babies? God knows where they are and they will pay. Many adults today have one thing on their minds and one thing only, and that is to have a good time in life.

A good time, many times, may be drinking, doing drugs, all kinds of sex. Most kids that are in State homes, their parents are on drugs, in prison or dead. Again I say they must answer to God in the end. No one, and I mean no one, will get by Him. I don't care who you are, or how wealthy you may be, we all must answer to God. No one can point fingers at some one else. Parents who are taking care of their children can not point fingers at the ones who are not, because we all have fallen short of God's Word. Many parents really do not know God, but they say they do. Deep down they do not know God because if they did, children would be in much better shape. Our court systems are over crowded with juveniles; it is so bad, law enforcement can not even control today's children. However, God can, and the parents He holds responsible for their children's actions.

Some parents have totally disobeyed the Word of God, and this is why children are so disobedient. They have respect for nothing and no one. Children are told to obey adults, but children are saying adults do not always do what is right. We live in a world now that adults will let children see them doing all kinds of ungodly things. All this is out of order with God, and again I believe children are not the problem, but adults are. Adults have society so badly messed up that only God can fix things. We as adults have destroyed everything that God has institutionalized because we think we are so smart. We are so smart until we will destroy this world. *"Who changed the truth of God into a lie, and worshipped and served the creature more than the creator."* (Roman 1:25-32). *"Children obey your parents in the Lord: for this is right. Honor thy father and mother; which is the first commandment with promise; that it may be well with thee, and thou mayest live long on the earth. And ye fathers, provoke not your children to wrath: but bring them up in the nurture and admonition of the Lord."* (Ephesians 6:1-4).

Parents have the responsibility of bringing their children up according to the laws of God, but adults have failed to do that. We have a war between adults and children. Every time a child commits a crime, the law wants to try him or her as an adult because they to do not know what to do with them. So just lock them up and throw away the key, this is the attitude our society has taken toward children. God's heart, my heart, and any saint's heart goes out to the children all over the world, because many of them do not have a chance in life, except their parents turn their heart to God. Children go into classrooms around this world everyday, and many of them do not know how they are going to be treated once they walk in that classroom. There are children young as 13 and 14 years old having sex with adult teachers. This involves male and female teachers alike, and it is very wrong of our adults. There is very little respect or trust between teachers and children. This is the case because teachers have done so many inappropriate things with, and in front of children over the years. There has become an immense gap between students and adult teachers. Children have acted out their anger by killing one another, or by killing Mom and Dad or other adults. When this happens our court system many times do not know how to charge them. It has come to pass many times that children are being charged for their crimes as adults from 12 years and older. It has become very sad that we live in a world where kids cannot be kids anymore.

We have come to an all time low as adults. God is very angry with us as a people, because we are a very sinful people disregarding His laws. People today do nothing but a lot of lip service.

It has been my experience on the job, many adults are always talking about having a good time, going to happy hour, doing a little drugs, also saying things such as, "I have to live my life!" They never want to learn about God. God is good, no, He is better than good, He is great! We never call on Him until we want things from Him. If you have no money in the bank, you cannot go to the bank expecting to withdraw money. The same with God, you cannot lie, steal, cheat, kill, hate, deceive, talk about people, misuse people, and think you are automatically going to Heaven to be with God when you die. God is love, kindness, joy, peace, and when I say God loves every man and woman, He does and wants them to turn their hearts to Him. He does not look at color. I do not care who tells you God looks at color, that person is a liar from the pit of hell, just like their father the devil. Children need loving church-going parents. Without this, children will not make it. We all need God in our lives. I read the newspaper, I watch the news on the television, I talk to people, and many times they are talking about the behavior of the parents and children. How the mother beat the child, the father sexually assaulted the girl, did you hear about the child that killed his parents last night? This is all we hear these days!

Just the other day on the news they were talking about how a father was driving down the street holding a two month old baby boy by one leg outside his car window. He then stopped the car, got out and threw the baby down on the cement. This precious baby never had a chance in his life. There are many more cases of abuse by parents all over this world, and it will get worse before the end of time.

These things do not worry me, or any other Christian because we know that God has said all these things must come to pass before the end of time. In that day God will not show mercy to the sinner. My heart goes out to all the abused children, and to the parents that were killed by their children. We must understand that when we choose to serve man instead of God, our life will be a living hell. Many of us have made the decision to do the will of man, and not God's will for their lives. Now, many of us suffer whatever comes our way because of bad choices. God is in control of the world and everything that is in it, but many of us choose not to obey Him. Our children have a long way to go in life, and many of them will never have a chance because of today's adults and parents. Many children will never see the inside of a church, because the parents will never take them.

This is part of the beginning of sorrows, but you do still have a chance. Give up the world, give up doing it man's way and do it God's way. For this is the right and only way, love your children with all your heart, do the right things in front of them. Take your children to church, and when you take them do not just drop them off, stay there with them. When the parent does not have prayer in the home on a daily basis, that home is unprotected, and Satan is free to go in and take over the home. Prayer changes things, and when we look to God for help and guidance this makes Him happy.

People are trying in every way to come up with ideas for children to have fun and entertainment, so that teen crime will go down. This will never happen because man does not have the answers for today's issues. The way to improve many of these problems is by living according to the Word of God and teaching the children by example.

Children can call 911 to report their parents for any reason! Parents have been stripped of their rights to raise their children. This has made God very angry with parents and society. All the answers are with God, but we choose not to follow Him. *"Set your affection on things above, not on things on the earth."* (Col 3:2) *"For to be carnally minded is death; but to be spiritually minded is life and peace. Because the carnal mind is enmity against God: For it is not subject to the law of God neither indeed can be."* (Romans 8:6)

We as adults are trying to beat the crisis that we are in, but everywhere man looks, he cannot find peace for his soul. Man is in a world of sin but he does not want anyone to know he has no answers for our troubles we face today. God wants man to call on him, but man is weak and too much like his father the devil. The devil has no good in him and he does not know how to be good. Blesses is the man that desires to walk and talk right before God. God teaches the adults how to love and to do good by their families. We must do what God wants us to if we want to win our children back from the devil. Jesus has paved the way for us by showing us how we should live, and teaching us how we should bring our children up. Jesus wishes for man to totally depend on Him, but we'd rather follow Satan. All the killing between children and adults will not stop because this has become a sin sick world. You walk and talk, but yet you are dying inside. You have become like the people of old, full of sin. Children see this and many of them copy the adult. Jesus desires that all men repent of their sins before it is to late for your own soul. *"For God sent not His son into the world to condemn the world; but that the world through Him might be saved. He that believeth on Him is not condemned, but he that believeth not is condemned already, because he hath not believed in the name of the only begotten Son of God. And this is the condemnation, that light is come into the world, and men loved darkness rather than light, because their deeds were evil. For everyone that doeth evil hateth the light, neither cometh to the light, lest his deeds should be reproved. But he that doeth truth cometh to the light, that his deeds may be made manifest, that they are wrought in God."* (John 3:17-21). *"Verily, verily I say unto you, he that believeth on me hath everlasting life."* (John 6: 47).

We believe as parents that we are the ones who make all the rules, and whatever we say goes. God has told us how to bring our children up, but we have made up our minds we are going to do it our way. Even as I write this book, I watch the news each night and it never fails, children killing parents, or parents killing children. It will not end until God comes, because parents have set the tone of disobeying God, and refuse to hear His voice. The world that we once knew is a thing of the past. Now that our children are so disobedient, we are wondering what went wrong? We have refused to obey or to do the will of God.

Dearly beloved, God wishes everyone would come to repentance while He is near. Turn from the works of the devil. Parents go back to being parents to your children. Obey God's law, do not be afraid to follow Him. He will guide you. It is God who has the power to give life or take it, physically and spiritually. Let us change our ways and be people that love God with all our heart, soul and mind, for this is right and pleasing to the Lord.

Pray with your children, have Bible study with them. Let us change our ways and call on God to bring us out of the mess we have gotten ourselves into. Amen.

CHAPTER THREE

Racism - How to Overcome It

"Thou shalt not hate thy brother in thine heart: thou shalt in any wise rebuke thy neighbour, and not suffer sin upon him. Thou shalt not avenge, not bear any grudge against the children of thy people, but thou shalt love thy neighbour as thyself. I am the Lord." (Lev.19:17-18). *"Ye have heard that it hath been said, thou shalt love thy neighbour and hate thine enemy. But I say unto you, Love your enemies, bless them that curse you, do good to them that hate you, and pray for them which despitefully use you and persecute you:"* (Matthew 5:43-44). *"No man can serve two masters: for either he will hate the one and love the other, or else he will hold to the one, and despise the other. Ye cannot serve God and mammon."* (Matthew 6:2-4).

We have lived in a world for generations where nothing exists but hatred and racism. Hatred brings on racism, racism brings on death. You have people that go to church every Sunday and they will tell you how much they love God, but yet they pack hatred in their heart for their fellow man. I want the world to know the God

I serve loves everybody all over the world. I've never been to an all Caucasian church, but I know some black people who have. They told me when they walked in the doors, they received the coldest look and some of the Caucasian members did not want to sit next to them. Yet they would sing the hymn, "What a friend we have in Jesus." This is not the way of God, but of the devil! For Jesus said, *"He that saith he is in the light, and hateth his brother, is in darkness even until now."* (1 John 2:9).

We live in a world of lies, cheating, killing, stealing and many more wicked things. A lot of these cruel things are in the church. We cannot, and will not, overcome racism until we as a people really get God into our lives. This problem has always existed among blacks and Caucasians. We have been waiting for many years on our leaders to bring blacks and Caucasians together, and this has not happened yet. It will never happen because the leaders are wicked themselves. They have no real understanding of love for all people, men only have love for themselves. Most of our leaders are Caucasian. Most all of the big corporations across the United States are owned by Caucasian men. Many times they do not have compassion, or want to deal fairly with other groups of people. The love for all mankind is not in his heart because he really does not know God almighty. It seems after all these generations that racism would have finally died, yet it is stronger than ever. This continues to occur because the devil is on the move using people of all colors. Anybody that will let him! We are a wicked and disobedient generation. You cannot hate a group of people and say you love God. You cannot call people names and say you love God. It is not right to hire people based on the color of their skin and then say you love God, you are a liar.

There is a proclamation in the Constitution of the United States, that was written by man, and it states that, "All men are created equal." The man that wrote that was a slave owner. The only words we can trust were spoken by God when He left with us the Holy Bible.

"The poor is hated even of his own neighbour but the rich hath many friends. He that despiseth his neighbour sinneth: but he that hath mercy on the poor, happy is he." (Provebs 14:20-21). *"These things I command you, that ye love one another. If the world hate you, ye know that it hateth me before it hated you."* (John 15:17-18). *"Marvel not, my brethren, If the world hate you. We know that we have passed from death unto life, because we love the brethren. He that loveth not his brother abideth in death. Whosoever hateth his brother is a murderer: and ye know that no murderer hath eternal life abiding in him."* (I John 3:13-15). *"If a man say I love God, and hateth his brother, he is a liar: for he that loveth not his brother whom he hath seen, how can he love God whom he hath not seen?"* (1 John 4:20) *"He that loveth his brother abideth in the light, and there is none occasion of stumbling in him, but he that hateth his brother is in darkness, and walketh in darkness, and knoweth not whither he goeth, because that darkness hath blinded his eyes."* (1 John 2:10-11).

Taking a wild guess, I would say about 93 percent of the world live the lie, "I hate no one," yet hatred is practiced each and everyday. God is real and we better wake up and realize that God is who we really need to make it in these last days. I know I don't have to tell many people this, but you don't know who to trust anymore. God is the only answer in these terrible times.

I was watching television one day and a black lady was being interviewed by another lady. The topic was racism. The black lady told the interviewer with tears in her eyes when she had to talk to her son about being treated different once he started school. When she began to talk about that I said, This will never happen to me," but it did. In 1991 racism was still alive, I had to tell my son how he would be treated once he started school. I told him he would be treated different from Caucasian children. When my children are in Sunday School they are taught God loves everybody the same. He does not have respect of persons, but yet they are treated different from Caucasian children by Caucasian teachers. Children of all races are confused by this big lie adults have taught them, "don't mix race." First of all, men were made by God and for God's purpose, God never speaks of race in the Bible. He call us Gentiles and Jews, and in the New Testament, Christians. Race comes from man not God. God loves all men the same. God has never said black or white, again it is Christians, Gentiles or Jews. We have let man burden us down with all his crooked ways. The people of the world need to return to God before it is too late. Confess your sins to Him so that you may really know Him. Racism is at the very heart of this world and no one wants to face up to it. We pretend it does not happen, but we know it is everywhere. It is in the White House, police departments, City Hall, schools, universities, and multi-race churches. Caucasian people spearhead it, I always wanted to know do they think other groups of people are just to lay down and be mistreated and never saying anything? There is no justice for the poor man there is no justice for men if they are not Caucasian. What is justice? What color is justice? Is justice for the rich and Caucasian? God is a just and fair God, every person is treated well by God, everyone is looked upon as somebody by him, we are wasting our time fooling with the foolish things of this world. We could have so much from God almighty. When I was younger, I was filled with hate because I was disliked from a child. I never understood why my parents went to back doors of restaurants to get our food. Sometimes I would go to the back with my mother and I would see all the Caucasian people sitting inside, eating, and having a good time. I would see bathrooms with signs that read, Colored and White. I saw drinking fountains that said the same. The colored fountains put out hot water while the white fountains put out cold water. I've seen black males beaten by Caucasian police, lied on, hung, and burned up by the Caucasian Klan.

What is so sad about all of this is the Caucasian men would get away with their bad deeds. The reason for it is many of your policeman, judges, lawyers, prosecutors are Klansmen themselves. Our parents would never say anything bad about them, so in my mind I was taught these acts were okay, but in the back of my childish mind something said no, it is not right.

Everything I saw was white, Jesus pictures were all white, Mary, mother of Jesus pictures were also white. As a kid you think this is the way the world was because your parents did not tell you any different, at least mine did not.

When I became a man, God was dealing with me in many ways. One of the things He let me know is that He does not love one group of people more than the other. No one knows what God looks like, so all these images men have made of Him, is a big lie.

As I write this book, we have an election coming up soon (Bush and Gore,) many people will go out and vote, looking for hope in these guys. I am here to tell you they have no answers for the world's problems, only God does. Racism is all over the world and world leaders cannot fix it. Israel and Palestine have been fighting over land for generations, and they are still fighting today over God's land.

We as a nation of people, dislike other people for no reason at all. I'd like for everyone that reads this book to go back in your mind and really think about why you dislike or hate someone. Is this because you have more money, better cars, a big home, because of skin color. Whatever the reason is for hating someone, it is stupid, and you are really the person with the problem. We told this lie that everyone is free in America, however some are free in America and some are still slaves.

We call racism a sensitive area. It is sensitive because deep down in our hearts, we know it is wrong, but we as a people love wrong more than right. God is about love and He loves all people It is too bad many of us do not believe or understand that, but it is true, God loves all people. Racism and hatred come from satan, and satan will work in whoever will let him. Satan is a killer, and a liar! Most of all he is a deceiver, and he has been deceiving mankind since the beginning of time. God is about truth, life, love, joy, and peace. So who are you haters, killers, liars serving when you do these bad things? Racism is not something God is a part of. He doesn't have anything to do with man not loving each other, but the devil does.

We as a people go around pretending we have love for one another, when we really do not. Many times people talk good in a person's face, and then stab them in the back. This is the kind of world we live in now, everyone pointing fingers at each other because of the problems of the world. All of our world leaders do not have any answers for these problems. We are a rebellious people looking and wanting answers for a dying world. God is our only answer, and besides Him there is no one else. However, God is not who we want! We'd rather look to men who cannot fix the world's problems. Things will not get any better in this lifetime, but they will get worse as time goes on. God understands that the world has so much to offer and tempt us with, but He wants us to depend and lean on him for all our needs. He knows what we need, and how to give us love for one another. Jesus is the real answer to all the world's problems. My son is in high school now, and one day we were talking about racial problems. He told me a Caucasian girl told him her parents told her to stay away from black people. He also told me there are Caucasian racist groups on his school campus. We talked about the young minds that have already been destroyed by hate, but you would be surprised at the number of young Caucasians that do not want to live with this hate for other people. Due to the love they have for their parents, they do what they are asked. In the meantime other parents must teach their children they will be treated differently in the Caucasian man's world, especially black males. They are watched very closely by the police. In God's world, everybody, I say that strongly, everybody is the same! They are equal. God loves the poor man just as much as He love the rich one. As a matter of fact, God said it would be hard for a rich man to enter into heaven, because many times rich people put there money ahead of God. Every man, woman, boy and girl need God, because we cannot make it without him.

We as a people have no interest in cleaning up racism, and do not know how to. People will not face up to the problem of racism, and they cannot fix it, only God can bring people together. With God all men are created equal! He treats them equally, and God loves all people the same. *"Whosoever hateth his brother is a murderer, and ye know that no murderer hath eternal life abiding in him."* (1 John 3:15) *"Beloved, let us love one another: for love is of God; and everyone that loveth is born of God, and knoweth God. He that loveth not, knoweth not God; for God is love. In this was manifested the love of God toward us, because that God sent his only begotten son into this world, that we might live through him."* (1 John 4:7-8)

Nobody wants to touch the subject of racism, but there are people who face it each and everyday. Many Caucasian people choose not to deal with the matter. People like living in darkness, they do not want to change because the devil will not allow them to. The devil hates, but God loves all people. Jesus said, *"Those who hate are just like their father the devil."* This He said to the hypocrites.

People are looking everywhere for somebody to unite us. I can remember when George W. Bush was running for president of the United States. They ran into a big mess in Florida, and this nation became divided. People were looking for Bush to bring us back together. They were looking to a man to bring people together and these politicians could not do it, and they still cannot bring people together.

It reminds me of the Jews in the Bible days. The Jews were looking for a great leader to come and deliver them. They had heard for years by the prophets of old that such a leader was coming. When Jesus came he was not accepted as their king because of the way he came. He was born poor, he was born in a stable, his family did not have money, so the Jews did not want him to be their king. They thought He was insignificant! People often look for big and great things from men but there is no good in them. Bush could not, and no other man can bring people together, the job is too big for man. We have a king, and His name is Jesus, and He is waiting for you to surrender your body, soul, and mind to Him. He will take care of the rest.

Racism will never go away because there will always be men that hate. It will only end after Jesus returns and gathers His saints. We have a king, and it is not any man on this earth. A Savior was born, and His birth was for all people, all over the world. *"For unto you is born this day in the city of David, a Savior, which is Christ the Lord."* (Luke 2:11) *"And the angel said unto them, fear not, for behold I bring you good tidings of great joy, which shall be to all people."* (Luke 2:10).

So you see, we have a king that loves all people, whether they are rich, poor, sinners, saints, black or Caucasian. It does not matter with Him. We are looking for true help in all the wrong places, when Christ is the answer, the only answer for this world.

The two greatest things we need in this world is more love and forgiveness. You cannot possess these things unless you have the love giver in you heart. I am not worried about racism, hatred, or unforgiving people, it is all in God's hand. God's Word say's, all men are created equal, and He loves us all the same. All the nasty names we call each other did not come from God. All the mean things we do to each other does not come from God. All the negative things come from the devil, he does not know any good. He gets in men's minds to do all the mean things that he does. God is about love, peace, joy and people helping other people. We need to stop putting our trust in men, and look to the hills where all our help comes from, which is Jesus Christ. He is waiting for people everywhere to just call on Him and turn their lives over to Him. He will be the potter, and you and I the clay. We do not live in a perfect world because all people are not fair and just, but God is. As a black man, I have seen a lot of unfairness is this world, but I have never looked to man to give me anything. All that I possess came from God. I give man no credit for the things that have happened in my life over the years. And over the years I have seen many ungodly things happen to black people. During slavery and even now, all blacks could, and can do, is cry out to the almighty God.

The children of Israel had to do the same thing when they were in bondage in Egypt.

God does not approve of hatred, mistreating other people, or when one person thinks they are better than another person. God used Moses, and Martin Luther King, Jr. to deliver His people out of bondage. As a kid, I saw how hard it was to achieve that freedom from racism, but God was not going to be denied. Dr. King lost his earthly life, but he received a crown of everlasting life through Jesus Christ. I understand that people of color still have to deal with racism. God will have the last word and not man. We must keep the faith, keeping, and trusting in God almighty, because all people have a right to the tree of life. We will never get rid of racism but we will forever have God. God is the only one who can do away with racism in our hearts, for he has all power. I have always noticed that leaders around this country say, "God bless America" at the end of their speeches. Ninety nine percent of these guys do not even know God, but they use God's name in vain. These words are also used to make people believe they are godly men. *"I said in my haste, all men are liars."* (Psalm 116:11) *"God forbid: yea let God be true, but every man a liar; as it is written, that thou mightest be justified in thy sayings, and mightest overcome when thou are judged."* (Romans 3:4) *"But evil men and seducers shall wax worse and worse, deceiving and being deceived."* (II Timothy 3:11) *"Ye are of your father the devil, and the lusts of your father ye will do. He was a murderer from the beginning, and abode not in the truth, because there is no truth in him. When he speaketh a lie, he speaks of his own: for he is a liar, and the father of it."* (John 8:44).

We are at a point and time in this world, you cannot, and I say that strongly, we cannot trust anyone but God. You only trust man as he follows God and does the will of God. All the ignorance of this world is wrong, and has always been wrong. God has never established or set in place racism. Neither hatred, economic troubles, etc. So let us all over the world turn from man and his wicked ways, and go back to God. This is the only way for us to make it. Amen.

Chapter Four:

A World of Sin

In today's society there is much deception taking place. Our world is filled with lying, cheating, unforgiveness, hatred, child abuse, domestic violence, women preachers, lust, no respect for one another, killing, rebellious children and wickedness. People can not be trusted anymore. There was a time when you could trust law enforcement, but they can no longer be trusted. In addition, we cannot trust our politicians, judges, or our government. Many of us around the world have sold our soul to the devil, by listening to man and his unwise laws; which he breaks himself each and everyday. We as a people can get hung up on what man can does for us, however, man is only out for what benefits himself, so God is angry with us. We have turned our faces from Him and turned to man, and all men will die and stand before God in that great and noble day. God has sent us so many warnings about man and his corruption, but we still love darkness rather that light.

The latest warning he has sent us was during the Bush and Gore election, you know and I know that was one big botch. I see Satan doing his job well. I've never seen so many lawyers and politicians lie backwards and forwards, corruptions was all over the State of Florida during the presidential 2000 election, and many of the people across the United States loved those lies that was laid out before them. God allowed the people to see how man can lie and have no conscious about it. Bush knew that he didn't win the Presidency, but wrong was on his side.

We are at a point where man has no shame about his wrongs, we all need to return to God's ways! All men must turn from their wicked ways, and seek those things that are righteous. We have lived in a society for years that is controlled by the Caucasian male. Many of the things he has done and said over the years, many of us thought it was gospel truth. I can remember when I was a little boy the Caucasian male had many black people believing that Jesus was a blue-eyed blonde. When I became a man, and was seeking God for myself, I found out that is not the case. Color does not matter to God for He loves all men equally. Some would say the Caucasian male owns everything on the earth, so Jesus must be Caucasian! Not so. I see black people as being like the Israelites, who were oppressed by the Egyptians for many years. We, as black people have been oppressed by the Caucasian race for many years, but God has always been there for all people. I can remember when the Republican Party was trying to put Clinton out of the White House for lying under man's oath. Those republicans that were trying to put Bill Clinton out for lying, had done a lot of lying themselves, they also had sexual affairs. When you point a finger at someone, you have got three more pointing back at you. Bill Clinton would not resign no matter how much they pressed him to. Clinton must have realized that God is his only true judge, and that God was the only one qualified to judge the people. It does not matter how much money one may have, everything on this earth belongs to God, and God alone. God set in place ten laws, thousands of years ago, and He has never broken one of His laws, and they are still the same this very day, but man breaks the laws of God each and everyday. We, the people of this world, have been overtaken with sin, because we have taken God out of our lives. We have taken Him out of the schools, out of the homes, out of the workplace. Going to church has become just a tradition for many. These are sad times, but there is hope through Jesus Christ.

I remember when I was in my twenties I had a drinking problem, and many times I would wake up the next morning and would not remember how I got home. I did not have any idea. Sometimes I would wake up from sleeping on the streets all night long. There were times I wanted to stop, and could not, because that old devil, satan had me boxed in. I stayed broke all the time, and people would talk bad about me behind my back, even people in my family ran my name down. I was a drunk for years with no help from any man or woman.

One day while sitting on my sofa thinking how sick and tired I was of living in the gutter. Man had failed me, so I decided to try Jesus. I remembered all my teachings that I received from my mother and grandparents. They saw to it we went to Sunday School every Sunday. All the good times suddenly started coming back to me while sitting there. I saw all the things God had done for them. I knew He could do them for me too.

One Thursday night I went to church. Standing outside was a preacher so I introduced myself to him. At first I did not tell him any of my problems I just wanted to hear him talk about how God loves sinners no matter what. After we finished talking I had a strong desire to be saved, and God did save me. God will forgive the sins of anyone who will draw nigh to Him. *"For whosoever shall call upon the name of the Lord shall be saved."* (Romans 10:13.) *"Stand, fast therefore in the liberty where**with** Christ hath made us free, and be not entangled again with the yoke of bondage."* (Galatians 5:1.) *"Verily I say unto you, except ye be converted, and become as little children, ye shall not enter into the kingdom of heaven."* (Matthew 18:3.) *"The Lord takes pleasure in them that fear him, in those that hope in his mercy."* (Psalm 147:10-11.) *"Casting all your cares upon him; for he careth for you."* (1 Peter 5:7) *"Blessed are the poor in spirit for theirs is the kingdom of heaven."* (Matthew 5:11.)

Jesus is the only way, He has all the answers. God loves all people, Black, Caucasian, Hispanic, Asian, rich, poor, and all sinners. All one must do is call upon the name of the Lord, it does not matter where you are, or what you have done in the past, He is just and faithful to forgive you, Jesus is not like man, unfair, unjust, untrustworthy, we need God more and more in our daily lives. Society must understand there is no hope in the men of this earth, if we put our hope in them, they have never lived up to anything that they promise. God can open doors for you that no man can close. God gives life, joy, peace of mind, and where there is hate, He brings love. God has all of this yet we will not put our trust in Him. It seems to me we place our trust in people who do not even know us. I am talking about people like the President of the United States, governors, senators, congressmen, and all these men want is to line their pockets with money, while you and I suffer deprivation. People want a way out of their hardships, but they will not give their lives over to God. *"Trust in the Lord with all thine heart; and lean not unto thine own understanding. In all thy ways acknowledge him and he shall direct thy paths."* (Proverbs 3:5-6)

I do not understand why so many of us will not give ourselves over to God, and this is sad. You like your life, and your sinful lifestyles. If we have faith that Jesus is always with us, we will better recognize Him in our daily living. We as a people should strive for the things that Jesus wants for our lives, instead we are striving for the things of satan, which will never do us any good. Jesus came to earth as a man to die for the sins of the world, yet we do not really care, our focus should be on God and His ways. No man can come to God except by Jesus Christ of Nazareth. Nothing comes easy in this life, but if you work for God, there is a great reward for you. *"And whosoever doth not bear his cross, and come after me, cannot be my disciple."* (Luke 14:27.)

God understands that we have so much to deal with here on this earth. He understands our sorrows better than any man, and He also understands there are so many wicked things to endure on this earth. But God wants us to understand that He has better things to offer, and He will give it to you freely if you would look towards Heaven and just say, "God I need you in my life," and give it over to

Him. But you must really mean it because God looks at the heart, and what God has to give lasts forever.

I often talk to my sixteen year old about things that are going on in the world. I can remember one conversation we were having one day. He told me the Caucasian children sit together in the cafeteria, Latinos all sit together, and Blacks sit together. What came to my mind was the turbulent 1950's and 1960's. I said to myself, here it is the twenty first century and hate is still as strong as ever. He also told me he talked to some of the Caucasian girls and they told him their parents taught them to dislike Black people. The girls would tell him they did not want to dislike people for no reason, but pressure from their parents made it hard to mix with Black people. This was hard for a sixteen year old to hear from these girls, but I think what hurt him more than anything was to see these girls trapped between their feelings, and what their parents wanted. I asked my son how did he feel about what the girls told him? He said you learn to deal with it and accept people for who they are. I told him, many things in this world you must learn to deal with, but do them through God. I have always said the adults of yesterday and today have made many things so bad for children of the twenty first century. Black parents must constantly tell their children as they grow up, "You will be treated different from Caucasian children, but no one is better than you, you can be whatever you want to be. Keep a low profile so cops won't look your way, especially Black males." These are the things Black parents have to say to their children, and it is fine, because God sees everything, and nothing gets by Him at any time. There is hope, but it is in Jesus Christ.

A school teacher came up to me one day and asked me would I come and speak to his class? He said, "Whatever you do, do not talk about God." This is sad to keep God out of our children's lives, but people have been doing this for years. It seems as if people of all colors are talking more and more about race relations, and problems that we face ahead. Children are so confused, they want to love one another, they want to love other races, but the adults have not learned how to ask the Love Giver to come into their lives, so they cannot talk about love to their children.

Parents in this day and age blame television for all the world problems, like violence, sex, cheating, lying, but I say it is because we, as a people, have gotten comfortable with today's way of life. It is not good for the adults or children not to think spiritual sometimes! We work hard for all kinds of material things, we look out for what we think is happiness, we work hard and play hard, year round and never give God any of our time. This is why we have so much sin in this world. We will not make it without the teachings and guidance of the love of Jesus Christ. Jesus wants to be your best friend in the time of trouble, He wants to be there when you feel there is no hope, but you have to learn to depend on Him for everything. You cannot stop on your own doing the worldly things, you do not have the power to overcome evil by yourself, it takes the will of God in your life. The devil would love to see us burn in hell with him, he knows there is no chance for him to live with God, but you and your children still have that chance. If you die in your own sins then in hell you will lift your eyes in vain. Many people think they can live any kind of way and still make it to heaven with God, but I want to serve you notice, that only the righteous shall see God and live with Him for evermore. I mean only those who have really turned there total life over to Him. However, the people of this world have a great desire to live a sinful life, and many adult call this the "good life," and have no conscious about the wrong they do. My God will hold every man and woman accountable for the things they do and say in their lifetime.

I now teach middle school children, ages 12, 13, and some 14 year olds. The school where I teach is like running a prison. The children are so out of hand, totally disturbing the class in every way they can. They curse like sailors, and there have been times when teachers catch children having sex in empty classrooms, while other students keep watch for them. I myself have seen girls and boys engaging in sexual activity in the school. You take the students to the office, and the office does not really want to deal with the situation because they already have a back log of referrals. You call the home, and ninelty percent of the time the child is being raised by a grandmother, who already has a hard time disciplining the child.

Then you have those children who tell you there mother is on drugs and is in prison, and so is my dad! And last of all you have those children who do have both parents at home, both parents are too busy giving the kid everything they want, and they forget they need to raise this child in a Godly manner. Some of the children will tell teachers, "My parents are afraid of me." Imagine little kids talking like this.

Teachers don't have time to teach anymore because they are constantly dealing with behavior problems. Many teachers quit right in the middle of a semester because they are afraid of the children. They feel they are not effective with the children, and it is a waste of time to try to teach them. Also you get no support from the front office, nor the School Board. Many children do these things because they know there is no consequences for their actions. Many of these children end up in trouble with the law, and then they find out the consequences are not like at school. There is about one thousand students at my school, and half of them have probation officers that come by and check on them once a month. All these children have been before judges, and adults are just turning there heads because they want the problem to go away on its own. It will not happen. Children of today have no respect or regard for anything, kids are basically raising themselves, because today's parents want someone else to do the job for them. Oh, but when you stand before the almighty God, parents will have to tell God why they failed their children, and you cannot lie to Him, He all ready knows.

I was told a large portion of children in this country are crack babies, mothers are doing drugs while carrying their babies. These women have no respect for their pregnancies, nor their bodies. This is what the world is faced with, a bunch of adults still trying to be children.

When Jesus come there will be no excuse for that kind of behavior, and the reason this happens is there is no prayer in the home, no going to Sunday School or church services period! Just party, party and more party! I feel children of today do not stand a chance to be productive men and women, because there is no focus by this society on eternal life. I want this world to know you are faced with eternal damnation if you do not change your ways. It is time right now to give your life to God, or there will be no hope for today's children and future adults. It does not matter how bad your life may be, God loves all sinners, and wishes you would just come to repentance. He does care about what you are doing with your life. He is just and faithful to forgive all sin. Hope, if you do not have Christ Jesus, tell me where is your hope? In the American flag? The American flag did not die for you, that is just an idol! God is your hope not man. Man is a liar, and only knows the truth if he really has God in his heart. In man there is no good, he has a sinful nature. But we as a people look up to man, and not our heavenly Father.

Poor people are often forgotten by the rich, the rich are in control and have no mercy for the needy, or the little man. If they did, the poor would be better off than what they are, but we can see that the poor are constantly overlooked by the men in power here on earth. People need to understand that man can't keep anything from you that God wants you to have. If man closes a door, God can open it, and the doors that men open, God can close. Many people lose their blessings because of their attitude towards God, which is not good. To be a child of God, your mind must be subject to His will, and it takes loving Him with all of your mind, all of your heart, all of your soul, and all of your strength. If I was not saved by grace and I did not know God, the world problems could depress me, or I would stay upset all the time, but when you really know God, you have a peace in Him that keeps you with a smile on your face. You need to take the Lord with you everywhere you go on the job, in your home, and when you are riding in your car you ought to have the Lord right next to you, this is the way He wants it, because God knows in the long run, every man, woman, boy and girl will need Him. Jesus died for mankind that He might have everlasting life. *"Ye are bought with a price; be not ye the servants of men."* (1 Corinthians 7:23.)

God does not want His people looking up to man for anything, because man does not have the power to give you eternal life, but we as a people get so wrapped up in material things, and these things of the earth will not last. Only what you do for Christ will last and that is why He has this deep concern for your life.

When I am sometimes watching television, you have certain channels that show girls posing naked, and they are only doing it for money and fame. These things will all vanish away, but hell is forever. *"For whosoever shall call upon the name of the Lord shall be saved."* (Romans 10:13.) It is better to trust in the Lord than to put confidence in man. It is better to trust in the Lord than to put confidence in princes. *"All nations compassed me about: but in the name of the Lord will I destroy them."* (Psalm 118:8-10.) I have been a poor man all my life, and I have never wanted to look up to man for anything, because I have known every since I could think, that there was no good in man and that he would lie about anything! This is because there is no God in him.

What is so great about this man Jesus Christ is that He is bigger than any king, president, or princes. This is the man who will never leave you nor forsake you. God will deliver you from all unrighteousness. *"Being then made free from sin, ye became the servants of righteousness."* (Romans 6:18.) *"But as many received him, to them gave he power to become the sons of God, even to them that believe on his name."* (John1:12.) Many people will tell you they believe in God in their own way, but yet they do sinful things. I understand people make mistakes, but no one should continue doing the things of the devil, but that is where we are talking good, looking good, but doing ungodly things all over this world. See, I had to put my trust in the Almighty God, because as I have always said man talks with a forked tongue in his mouth. The forefathers of this country have said all men are created equal, well from a little boy to a man, I have not seen equality, as a matter of fact, just the opposite. The Black man has never been treated equal by the Caucasian man, and I say never strongly. Man has been a hypocrite from the time he came on this earth, this is why I do not put any hope or trust in any man on this earth. God has proved Himself to me, time after time. I know with all my heart and soul that Jesus Christ loves me just for who I am, and in Him is true equality. *"Love not the world, neither the things that are in the world. If any man love the world, the love of the father is not in him. For all that is in the world, the lust of the flesh, and the lust of the eyes, and the pride of life is not of the father, but is of the world."* (John 2:15-16).

God cannot use you when you have your eyes on things that man has to offer, which many times are sinful things. Remember in the garden of Eden, Eve had the lust of the eyes, everything that look good is not good, for she had to learn that the hard way. Because of her lust we must die that first death, Adam sold us out to sin, but God had so much love for us that he let his Son die on the cross for our sin. One man sold us out to death, and another man (Jesus) came to give life.

Pride is a killer and we live in a world now where pride has overtaken people, nobody today wants to be humble. Everyone is looking to get to the top. We have so much road rage; many people trying to win the lottery; gays wanting the right to marry. All of these things are because the love of God is not in many people anymore, and that is because people think this world is their home, but I want you to know there is a Heaven and hell. *"If we say that we have no sin, we deceive ourselves, and the truth is not in us. If we confess our sins, He is faithful and just to forgive us of our sins, and to cleanse us from all unrighteousness."* (John 1: 8-9). There is thousands of people that go to church every Sunday, they go to weekly activities at church, and yet they deceive themselves each and everyday, while confessing they know God. But, they do the things of the devil, you cannot be a curser and say you love God! You cannot hate people and say you love God. You cannot be a liar, and say you love God, for all these are wicked acts. This is what I like about God, He will forgive you of all your sins that you have committed if you only stop deceiving yourself. *"For whosoever shall call upon the name of the Lord shall be saved."* (Romans 10:13). *"And it shall come to pass, that whosoever shall call on the name of the Lord shall be delivered."* (Joel 12:32).

We are talking here a lot about being saved, this is what it is all about with God, God sees, and knows, we are in danger of hell fire, and He is trying to free us from hell fire before death comes knocking at your door, and it will one day. This is one appointment no one will break, death is at God's timing, not man's, so what is happening is God wants everyone on this planet earth to have their opportunity to have this eternal life, and that only comes by truly being saved. *"Verily I say unto you, except ye be converted, and become as little children, ye shall not enter into the kingdom of heaven."* (Matthew 18:3). "No man can serve two masters: for either he will hate the one, and love the other; or else he will hold to the one, and despise the other. Ye cannot serve God and mammon." (Matthew 6:24). There are people who wants to do the things of the world and also serve God, and it does not work that way. To serve God, you must totally yield to Him and His ways, because He knows what is best for your life. As I was saying earlier in the book, pride will send many people to hell for the simple reason they are not going to drop their pride, and humble themselves as little children to God. They would rather serve God part time, and the devil the other half, well I am here to tell you it won't work! God does not need us, but we need Him. That is why there are so many backstabbing people in the world, play your friend, play someone else's friend, talk about you behind your back, talk about someone else behind their back. So you cannot say you love God, when you do the works of the devil. God doesn't need us, trying to keep the devil happy and Him too, is not possible, you must come all the way clean with God, or stay away nasty. God does not have room in His kingdom for pretenders. God has given us warning after warning in His Word, yet we continue with our old sinful nature.

When Noah was building the ark, he also was preaching to the people to repent before it is too late, but they made fun of him and just laughed, until the day he and his family went into the ark. It was a sad day when God Himself brought destruction upon the earth with a flood. The people were not laughing anymore at Noah for they wanted Noah to let them into the ark, but God said, no, you had your chance to come out of your sin, but you were hard-hearted, rebellious, people, lovers of pleasures more than God. You were high minded, deceitful, you loved serving the devil more than God, now in hell you will lift your eyes with your father the devil.

We should want to be in Christ, for the world's things are only for a little while, they don't last forever, but hell and Heaven will always be here. If I did not put my hope in Christ, I would not be who I am today, while I was a sinner, I told the world goodbye and hello the Holy Ghost. Dealing with man you stay depressed, man is always letting you down, you have more sadness than joy, you cannot find peace, and don't think for a minute just because some people are rich they are happy all the time, believe it or not, they have more problems than poor people. They just know how to hide their feelings in public. *"If in this life only we have hope in Christ, we are of all men most miserable."* (1 Corinthians 15:19). So you see I am looking for something bigger and better from Christ, He said it was and I believe in Him, so I do not have hope in this life but the next life The Bible talks about. *"Therefore if any man be in Christ, he is a new creature: old things are passed away; behold all things become new."* (II Corinthians 5:17). *"I am the true vine, and my Father is the husbandman. Every branch in me that beareth not fruit he taketh away: and every branch that beareth fruit he purgeth it, that it may bring forth more fruit. Now ye are clean through the word which I have spoken unto you. Abide in me, and I in you. As the branch cannot bear fruit of itself, except it abide in the vine no more can ye, except ye abide in me."* (John 15:1-4).

I am now saved and filled with the Holy Ghost, my job calls for me to help my brothers and sisters that are not in Christ to come to repentance. I have been purged by Him to do His will, and I now understand that God truly has a deep unconditional love for me, and the world (satan) is not my friend, he only come to steal, kill, and destroy. The most important thing he wants is to destroy your mind! If he gets the mind, your body will follow, it could be alcohol, smoking, drugs, sex. *"For as much then as Christ hath suffered for us in the flesh, arm yourselves likewise with the same mind: for he that hath suffered in the flesh hath ceased from sin; that he no longer should live the rest of his time in the flesh to lusts of men, but to the will of God."* (1 Peter 4:1-2). *"But the end of all things is at hand: be ye therefore sober, and watch unto prayer. And above all things have fervent charity among yourselves: for charity shall cover the multitude of sin."* (1 Peter 4: 7-8).

People want God in their lives, but they are not willing to suffer for Him in the flesh. Jesus suffered all the way to the Cross in the flesh, many rich people would have you believe God does not love the poor, or black people. This has been the story for years, but Jesus did suffer at the hand of sinners. But I want you to know He did rise on the third day, and He also rose in my life in a 1977. God is no fool, He knows why so many people are not serving Him with their whole heart, because they are always looking for the world's goods, which are not good for your soul, and neither shall the worldly goods last forever. Everything with man is just a matter of time.

The lust of the world will destroy men and women of all races, because lust of the eyes has overtaken them. When the Lord has had enough of our sinful ways, He is just to send us a warning before he destroys. In the book of Amos, God saw the wickedness of Israel, and to change their ways or He would destroy them. Israel didn't listen to the warning. It took some years, but He did destroy them all. God himself once again saw the wickedness on the earth, and He is very angry about what is happening on the earth right now. Gay's wanting to marry each other is one example that is an abomination before God. There is police corruption in every state, city and town. Also women calling themselves preachers, and man allowing them to do it.

Parents are not raising their children, children are raising themselves, everything is about money, and man does not care how he gets it or who he hurts or lies to, as long as he gets what he wants. Women wanting to be like men, and men wanting to be like women, and television is so corrupt this day and time you cannot hardly allow your children to watch it, but parents do, just to keep the kid out of their hair.

America is a big hypocrite, always wanting to bring unity in some other country when there is no unity in America. We are just pretending to get along, and as I have always stated, racism is alive and well in these United States, and it is not going away until Jesus comes back. *"Hear this word that the Lord hath spoken against you, O children of Israel against the whole family which I brought up from the land of Egypt, saying you only have I known of all the families of the earth: therefore I will punish you for all your iniquities."* (Amos 3:1-2).

God has put up with your filth for generations, your indecent, obscene gross moral corruption, and He is taking people out of here each and everyday. People are dying in their sins because they love the lusts of this world more than God, and it is very sad. When people die, I hear other people say, well she or he is gone to a better place, or they will say Heaven. Now when you serve the devil and do not do the will of God, you are not going to Heaven, but hell is where you will live, for you cannot serve the devil and think you are going to be with the Lord. *"But let none of you suffer as a murderer, or as a thief, or as an evil doer, or as a busybody in other men's matters. Yet if any man suffer as a Christian, let him not be ashamed; but let him glorify God on this behalf. For the time is come that judgment must begin at the house of God and if it first begin at us, what shall the end be of them that obey not the gospel of God? And if the righteous scarcely be saved, where shall the ungodly and the sinner appear?"* (1 Peter 4:15-18).

Chapter Five

The Corruption of Adults - Working Parents

We now live in a world where dads and moms are trying to make more money. This has become a way of life in our so-called perfect world, and serving the Lord is nowhere in the plans of men and women. You have your ordinary women who want children, but not the dad, then you have your career women who want children also, but not the dads. They bring these children into the world and want someone else to take care of them. There are so many children in the system today it is sad, you have those moms who have abortions or put them up for adoption. There are moms who leave their new born babies in trash cans; I know this one mom who left her baby lying in the snow, they also leave their babies on someone else's porch. You have many children in the school system that are crack babies, the whole time the mom was carrying the child she was doing drugs, so once these children grow up they end up on medication. Many times while in the classroom some students have to be excused to go to the nurse to take their medication, so they do not get upset in the classroom. We wonder why there is so much misbehavior in society and the school system from children. Many times the moms do not know where the dad is, and the dads do not want to be found. The so-called dad does not want to take any kind of responsibility for the children they father, as a matter of fact when a woman lets a man know she is going to have his baby, the first thing he wants is a DNA test. Sometimes they have good reason, for many girls in this day and time sleep with two different guys in the same day and think nothing of it. Where are the real men? Children do not stand a chance these days. God put the man as the head of the family. Many men in this society do not want that role or they are not stepping up to the plate as real men. Instead they want the woman to take the role as the head, if both my grandfathers could see what women are bringing into this world nowadays as men, it would make them sick. God is not happy about how men have tried to destroy what He has instituted between man and woman. Nowadays men want to marry men, women want to marry women, and all this is satan's doing. God sees it all and He will have the last word. God left instructions for parents concerning raising their children, but many parents choose do it their way.

This is why children are so disobedient, they do not know who they are, what is okay or what is not. Adults have them so confused. Their little minds cannot contain all the things some adults say is okay, other adults say certain things are not okay. Sadly today our teens see an alarming number of dysfunctional families. On a daily basis, they come face-to-face with people from broken homes and shattered lifestyles. When teens recognize their own family structure is crumbling they may feel worthless, unloved, misunderstood, and alone. They may even be physically abused. Children even start killing their parents, or have them put in jail! Children lose respect for adults when they find out adults do not deal straight. It's easy to understand, then, why some of our children may have turned to drugs, destructive peer groups, premature sexual relationships, and materialism. They're looking for acceptance. Sadly so, they do not know God loves them because the adults in their lives are not church goers. Adults of today are not following the instructions of God. *"Train up a child in the way he should go: and when he is old, he will not depart from it."* (Proverbs 22:6).

God understands children will get into other things while they are growing up, but if the adults did things according to God's law and not man's law, children would not be in the shape they are in today. *"Foolishness is bound in the heart of a child; but the rod of correction shall drive it from him."* (Proverbs 22:15). There is nothing wrong with bringing out the belt every now and then, but we think we know more than God, so instead we believe in "time out." *"Withhold not correction from the child: for if thou beatest him with the rod, he shall not die. Thou shalt beat him with the rod, and shalt deliver his soul from hell."* (Proverbs 23:13-14). The rod will put a certain amount of fear in the child before they do something wrong, because they will know mom or dad might pull out the belt. The belt brings fear, "time out" does nothing, this is why children have no fear of anything, not even God's or man's law. As long as parents disregard the laws of God, to follow what man says concerning raising your children you will forever bring up ungodly children. When God is not in your life there is no hope for them, or you. These are the last days, and the Bible must be fulfilled, children are going to get worse not better. Parents are not going to bring up their children to know the way of God, and this is sad. Parents will not change, because they like what they are doing and the children are the ones who suffer. Children need a chance in life, they need real love from real people who love God also, parents who put their needs first, no matter what the parent may have going on in their lives. Above everything else parents need to take their children to Sunday School. This is not happening in many families. Parents should see putting their children in Sunday school as more important than any public school. Public school is only good for a while on this earth, but where will your child's soul appear on that great day? You see, this natural life is only for a season, but eternal life is forever. Many parents see their children day after day, however they really do not have a clue what their child is into, or what their child is thinking. Children need more attention than they often receive from their parents, it is impossible to adequately know one's child, or children, that's why we must do the things the way God has commanded us to do. That is why He said train them up in the way they should go.

My father in Heaven is looking down to earth, and He is not happy with the way children are being raised. As a result of His disappointment He has cursed the earth and He has done what no man can change but God. You can go on believing the government can bring families together, it will never happen. Modernization and education are driving people of this world straight to hell with their father the devil. If you do not have a job at all, will you make a pay check? Can you make a withdrawal if you have not put any money in the bank? The same with God, if you have not given Him your total life, you cannot go back with Him to Heaven when He comes the second time. If you never take your children to Sunday School or church period, to hear the Word of God, how can you expect the child to know God and to do things God's way and not the devil's way? Parents need to wake up and understand how they are hurting their children by not teaching them about God. God should be first in every home, not just in words, but in actions as well. God wants everyone to enjoy the best life possible, He wants all of us to lead full, rich lives, and experience his love. (Jeremiah 31:3).

But, we as a people have rebelled against God, and are living sinful lives before His face. When this happens your sins separates you from God forever. *"For all have sinned and fallen short of the glory of God."* (Romans 3:23). Futhermore, we deserve to pay a penalty because we sinned. (Roman 6:23). Only God could solve our problems with sin, and this He did. He loved us so much he sent his Son, Jesus, to die, paying the penalty each of us deserved. (John 3:16,17). You are not forced to accept God's solution, to apply Jesus' payment for sin to your life, you must personally commit yourself in belief to Him. Satan has done nothing but lied and mistreated you all your life, and keep you in danger of hell's fire. You must look to the hills from whence cometh your help, it all comes from God. If you declare openly that Jesus died for your sins, and believe that God raised him from the dead, God has promised you eternal life. (Romans 10:9; 1 Corinthians 15:3,4; 1 John 5:11). As you study the Bible and talk with God through prayer, you will grow closer to Him and enjoy the full life he intended. (John 10:10). Now some people that have plenty of money, or that are rich, will tell you they are living the good life and that they do not need anything from God. Those are foolish people, what is on this earth only lasts for a little while, and I have never seen a U-Haul trailer behind any rich man's hearse, you will take nothing from this earth with you but your own soul, and that will be judged by God, not the devil whom you now serve.

People talk good and act like godly people, for you really do not want other people to see what you are really about, so we pretend with another face. Consequently we do not fool God because He knows each and every man's heart. The time will come when God is more important than all jobs, more important than money, more important than any material thing you may possess, but at that time it just may be too late for you. God is not on your time, you are on His time. Children all over this world are crying out for love, longing for real parents that will do the right thing by them. The parent's children have turned to the System for help. The System has turned to the System, but no one is turning to God for help. He is the only one that can help you through your troubles in this world. Parents, you have your careers going, and you still are not satisfied, you want more! This is the way the devil wants you to think, so he can have access to your children's mind. While parents continue to better their careers, their children are being taken over by the devil. When children have not had God instilled into their lives, they will do whatever their little minds tell them to, and many times the devil is in control.

The Bible must fulfill itself, the Word of God is manifesting itself through Jesus Christ, our Lord and Savior. Now Jesus stands for righteousness, and all that He does is good, so the next time you do evil ask yourself, is it from Lord? Adults are totally sin sick, and many people are drowning in their own sins. Jesus has come and shown man what it takes to get to Heaven. He has told us through His Word how we must live on this earth. Men and women all over the world, not just one race of people, but all people think they are able to help God to solve the world's problems. The world's problems were here before we got here, and they will be here well after we are gone. *"Seek ye the Lord while He may be found, call ye upon Him while He is near, let the wicked forsake his way, and the unrighteous man his thoughts: and let him return unto the Lord, and He will have mercy upon him; and to our God, for He will abundantly pardon."* (Isaiah 55:6-7). There will come a time in your life when you will want to seek God, you may be in the hospital, on your death bed, in prison, and God is no longer near for you, that will be a bad day in your life. You, the wicked, need to let your thoughts become holy thoughts, but that cannot happen until the potter comes into your life. God knows and sees all things.

I was watching a program one day called, Court TV, these three girls had robbed eight stores. Believe it or not, they were all young teenagers and all three were on drugs! One mother was being interviewed on television, she was asked whether she knew if her child was doing drugs. She was also asked the number of times she talked to her daughter about drugs. She responded the topic had been discussed many times. Now her daughter was on her way to jail with her friends. These are the kinds of things that go on between parents and children when you do not center your life around God, you are going to have big problems. It is very important to put God in your children's lives, and the way to do that is to take your children to Sunday School, and to mid-day Sunday services. When you do not, you are telling the devil it is okay to have a hold on my child's life. Adults have taken all the Godly things from their children, such as, prayer out of the home, prayer out of the public school, they do not go to Bible study one day a week. Families do not sit down to dinner together and pray together anymore, parents are not talking about God with their children on a daily basis. There are even some parents who tell their children not to talk about God in public, this is why children are ending up in the courts, in jail, and in the cemetery at such early ages. God spoke to me one day and told me parents would be spending a lot of time in the courts and cemeteries, and it is happening all over the world. God cannot lie and He will have the last word, I think corruption has set up in the heart and soul of many adults. Many adults have done things their way so long and have lied so many years, that they now live in denial. I'd like to say to those of you that want to overcome the sins that are in your lives, Christ has been waiting upon you to call His name all your life. In these last days, He is the only one that can restore your home, your children, and your mind. We are living in a time where parents will constantly give over to satan, but God wishes that you would come to repentance. Many working parents feel guilty about how they treat their children, so they make it up by giving them money. Your children are not looking for money or material things, they are crying out for their parent's support, and most of all their love. There should be many things parents should focus on in raising their children, but the main focus should be to teach them to love God with all their mind, all their heart, all their soul, all their strength. This is the first commandment of God.

Children go to school each and everyday feeling low and feeling there is no way out for them. If they only knew how much God really loves them, wants to help them and to be a part of their life. Yes, the Father can take away the pain from children and parents, He is just that kind of God. We must first admit to ourselves that we need God, and admit that He is the author and finisher of our faith.

Single Parents:

Many say children living with one parent have it the hardest in life, that they are victims of divorced parents, parents who never got married, but who like having sex together. Dad may be in prison or dead, and Mom may be in prison or dead. Children who live with both parents many times watch them fight among themselves, especially the ones that do not pray in the home. The children love both parents, so it is hard for them to take sides. When I was growing up in the fifties and sixties, if couples broke up, many times the child was awarded to the mother. However, times have changed now, so many mothers are unfit to raise their children, so Dads are receiving custody. Many fathers are doing a good job raising their children alone, and there are women who just do not want to be mothers. This is the kind of world we are in now, many adults have made their minds up to do things their way, and consequently children are suffering.

Single parents are working all day, and the children are responsible for themselves when school is out. They are free to do whatever they please until the adult gets home, so the crime rate is up, the death rate is up among teens. By the time parents realize their child is out of hand, it is too late, and the way many parents find out their child is having problems is through their involvement in criminal activity, death, or the child starts trying to fight the parents themselves. One thing I am tired of hearing parents saying, is that they need help with their child. They also say they cannot do anything with their child. Parents have to raise their children according to God's will. No matter how much we want things to change with adults and children, it will not, until we believe in the laws of God, we as a people do the will of this world, not of God, and this is why your children are hitting you, talking back to you, and have no respect for you whatsoever. God is the answer to all your problems, and until we understand that, believe that, and live by His Words, parents and children are damned by God. You have become a rebellious people, too high minded for God, but Jesus is saying, will you come while the blood is yet running warm in your veins, while your are clothed in your right mind, but adults are too wrapped up in the goods of this world. Children need more than money, they need more than promises from Mom and Dad. They need you, the parent, above everything they need adults in their little lives who love God, and who will take them to Sunday School.

God knows the depression and unhappiness of all children around the world. Many single moms today bring men into their homes to shack up with them and their children. The children do not like that because it is not their biological parent. Some children address this to the single parent, and other children say nothing, but totally dislike the setup. The parents do not listen, nor do they care how the child feel about the live-in mate.

Many single moms and dads work so hard during the week, and some of them work seven days a week, so this means they do not have time for the child. They do not leave time in their schedules to take the child, or children, to church! When this happens, the parent has no control of the child because they have not been the parent they should have been. I want every adult to know, God will see you in the Judgement for your disobedience in raising your children. All the things you now suffer and go through will not get better as long as sin is in your life. *"All unrighteousness is sin, and there is a sin not unto death."* (1John 5:17). *"We know that whosoever is born of God sinneth not; but he that is begotten of God keepeth himself, and that wicked one toucheth him not."* (1 John 5:18).

There are two births in a person's life, not just one! One is earthly and the other is spiritual. Some people choose to be nonbelievers, because they like sin and do not want to really give up the wordly things in their lives. When you become a believer, you want God to save you from your sins, and to forgive you for all unrighteousness, then you become His child, and you are born again spiritually. This is the second birth through Christ Jesus. You keep yourself Godly, and stay away from wicked things through the power of Jesus Christ, Our Lord and Savior of the world. *"The sting of death is sin; and the strength of sin is the law."* (1Cor. 15:56). *"For the wages of sin is death; but the gift of God is eternal life through Jesus Christ our Lord."* (Romans 7:23). *"If we say that we have no sin, we deceive ourselves, and the truth is not in us, if we confess our sins, He is faithful and just to forgive us our sins, and to cleanse us from all unrighteousness. If we say that we have not sinned, we make Him a liar and His word is not in us."* (1 John 1:8-10).

Where ever you are right now? Just stop what you are doing and tell God you are a sinner and that you no longer want to live in sin. Tell God you believe Jesus died for your sins and He rose on that third day. God will come into your life. What I like about this is God loves me for myself with no hidden agendas, and He does not look down on you because you are poor, or because you are a sinner. God loves us so much. Children need saved moms and dads, it does not matter whether you are a couple or single. If you bring your children up in the way of the Lord, they will start to see you differently and begin to obey you.

Divorced Couples:

Couples are getting divorces these days just like changing clothes, not looking at how it hurts their children, or their mate. We see everyday that this world does not respect marriage, or the vows the couples take! Marriage means nothing, divorce means everything. Couples are saying we will try marriage, but if my spouse makes me mad, gets on my nerves, or if we see the marriage is not going anywhere, we will get a divorce. Marriage is honorable before God, God Himself instituted marriage for man and woman. Once couples start having problems in their relationship they think the first thing they should do is get a divorce, instead of trying to work things out. That is why when I hear couples saying how much they are in love with one another, I see the true person when problems in the relationship come up. This is the devil's job to break up homes and marriages. Divorces can be a mess, not only does the devil want couples to break up, he would love for them to kill each other or make each other's lives miserable. Many times he wins because the adult does not have God in their life. Divorce brings on child support, one adult moves out of the house, and most times tempers get out of hand. If there are children, they are split between both parents, everything between the couple becomes split up. All these things are the works of the devil, not God. God wishes couples would sit down and work their problems out. Most all, God would love for couples to call on Him, and ask Him to help them. People would rather do what satan wants them to do, and that is to leave their family. Oh, wicked generations, it is time to call on God. *"It hath been said, whosoever shall put away his wife, let him give her a writing of divorcement: But I say unto you, that whosoever shall put away his wife, saying for the cause of fornication, causeth her to commit adultery: and whosoever shall marry her that is divorced committeth adultery."* (Matt 5:31).

The Pharisees also came unto Jesus, tempting him and saying unto Him, Is it lawful for a man to put away his wife for every cause? And He answered and said unto them, *"Have ye not read, that he which made them at the beginning made them male and female, and said for this cause shall a man leave father and mother, and shall cleave to his wife: and they twain shall be one flesh? Wherefore they are no more twain, but one flesh. What therefore God hath joined together, let no man put asunder."* They say unto him, Why did Moses then command to give a writing of divorcement, and to put her away? He saith unto them them, *"Moses because of the hardness of your hearts suffered you to put away your wives: but from the beginning it was not so. And I say unto you, whosoever shall put away his wife, except it be for fornication, and shall marry another, committeth adultery: and whoso marrieth her which is put away doth commit adultery."* (Matt

19:3-9). *"It is good for a man not to touch a woman. Nevertheless, to avoid fornication, let every man have his own wife, and let every woman have her own husband."* (Matt 7:1-2).

Now when a couple get married they are no longer two, but one, in the sight of God they are one flesh, so that mean that they are never to leave each other unless it is death. If one of the mates cheat on the other, God wish you forgive that mate, but by God's law you are free to leave. Due to the hardness of man's heart, Moses gave them a writing of divorcement, and that is how it is today. People are hard hearted, no forgiveness for their spouse, and no one else. So you see God is not for divorce, He wishes that every couple, man and woman would work their differences out. I wish that all men and women really knew God, the Father, and would let Him have their lives. If we would give God control of our lives, sin would not overtake us. God is not in divorces, but the devil is. God does not cause divorces, but the devil does. God would love for all marriages to be prosperous. Looks like many people all over this world would rather serve their father the devil. We are in a time when adults of this world have no regard for anything to do with morals. Children are getting the short end of the stick because most parents are not giving them what they really need. What all people need is God Almighty in their mind and soul. Sex is destroying so many homes and lives. Women are using their bodies for power, money and fame. They don't care what man they use, as long as he has plenty of money. Women do not care if men are married as long as the money is there. Men are still failing God behind women. They are falling in the trap of a woman's body and face. Man is so stupid, he will give up everything he has for five minutes of pleasure with a woman. Again, the children suffer when the home is broken up by the couple. There are men losing their jobs because of sex with women. All these things are the works of the devil, to bring men down and if he can succeed, he feels God will have been defeated because God's glory is man. I want the whole world to know God will have the last word. Men are selling their souls to the devil for little or nothing, not realizing what they are doing. Thank God for Jesus, that with His death for a lost world we now have a chance to get things right in our lives. God is the only one that can control satan, no man can fight the devil on his or her own, and expect to overcome, but the name of Jesus Christ will drive him away. Men are walking away from their families for any kind of reason, but the biggest reason is sex. It is not good for children to be caught up in the mess adults created, God wishes that His people would turn their face to Him, call upon His holy name. He wants you to draw nigh to him while the blood runs warm in your veins. I know some people say to themselves, "Why does God let so many bad things happen to families?" What people must understand is when you do not allow God to be the head of your life, when you do not go to church, or take your children to church, and when you do not pray in the home, and above all, when you are disobedient to God, that means the devil is the head of your life! This is why there are so many marriages breaking up.

Homosexuals:

"God created man in His own image, in the image of God created he him; male and female created he them. (Gen. 1:27), and God caused a deep sleep to fall upon Adam, and he slept: and He took one of his ribs and closed up the flesh instead thereof, and the rib, which the Lord God had taken from man, made he a woman, and brought her unto

the man. And Adam said, this is now bone of my bones, and flesh of my flesh: she shall be called woman, because she was taken out of man. Therefore shall a man leave his father and his mother, and shall cleave unto his wife: and they shall be one flesh. And they were both naked, the man and his wife, and were not ashamed." (Gen. 2:21-25). *"But from the beginning of the creation God made them male and female."* (Mark 10:6). Homosexuals have no rights when it comes to same sex relationships, because God is totally against this practice, God made them male and female. There are homosexual demons, just like there are lying demons, hateful demons, and that is just to name a few. There are many kinds of evil demons of this world. God never made man for a man. Man's own lust has driven him to do these evil things. Now, God loves all homosexuals just like he loves all liars, but he just does not like the sin they engage in. So when you see a man with another man or a woman with another woman, they are sin sick. Have you read the Bible, really read it? You see, God did not ordain same sex relationships. God sees this as perverted, and not right in His sight. I do not care how many laws are passed, or who said it is okay, it is a sin before God Almighty. *"Know ye not that unrighteous shall not inherit the kingdom of God? Be not deceived: neither fornicators, nor idolaters, nor adulterers, nor effeminate, nor abusers of themselves with mankind."* (1 Corinthians 6:9). God has nothing to do with people of the same sex dating or marrying one another. God calls it abusing themselves, and I say this very strongly, homosexuals will take their place in hell when that great day comes. God Himself will put all sin under His feet in the judgment. Man is trying to find a cure for Aids, and there will never be one. God will not allow there to be one, this is a punishment from God because man with his sinful ways have tried for generations to turn God's work dirty and he will not win. God would love for mankind to turn from homosexuality to following His word. I have talked to many homosexuals in my time, sometimes the talks would be general, and other times we would talk about the Lord. This would give me the chance to minister to them, but I would always hear the same old excuses, I want to stop, but I can't. This is the work of the devil to confuse the mind, and it works when they do not have God in their life. Let no one fool you, homosexuals are not going to Heaven to be with the Lord. You must be born again, God will not tolerate sin. It has become very sad that children are living in homes with homosexual parents. It does nothing but confuse their little minds. Adults, if you want to be homosexual that is one thing, but to bring little children into your mess is not pleasing to God. When they go to school and there little friends find out they have same sex parents, they are confused and this is what happens to the whole world, it is confused. So what we have today in our society is a lot of children confused about who is right among the adults. Children are left to struggle with which lifestyle is actually the correct one to live? But the Bible say's, *"Thou shalt not lie with mankind, as with womankind: it is abomination."* (Leviticus18:22-23). *"Wherefore God also gave them up to uncleanness through the lust of their own hearts, to dishonour their own bodies between themselves."* (Romans 1:24-28). *"Whosoever lieth with a beast shall surely be put to death."* (Exodus 22:19). There is only one who is perfect and just, God Almighty. The word of God is the only thing that will stand in the end.

CHAPTER SIX

It's About Jesus

"Who hath believed our report? And to whom is the arm of the Lord revealed? For he shall grow up before him as a tender plant, and as a root out of a dry ground: He hath no form nor comeliness; and when we shall see Him, there is no beauty that we should desire Him. He is despised and rejected of men; a man of sorrows, and acquainted with grief: and we hid as it were our faces from him; he was despised and we esteemed him not. Surely he hath borne our griefs, and carried our sorrows: Yet we did esteemed him stricken, smitten of God, and afflicted. Jesus Christ was wounded for our transgressions, he was bruised for our iniquities: the chastisement of our peace was upon him, and with his stripes we are healed. All we like sheep have gone astray, we have turned every one to his own way; and the Lord hath laid on him the iniquity of us all. He was oppressed, and he was afflicted, yet he opened not his mouth: he was brought as a lamb to the slaughter, and as a sheep before her shearers is dumb, so he openeth not his mouth." (Isaiah 53:1-7).

Isaiah was one of God's prophets, and God wanted him to foretell of Jesus coming. Isaiah told what He would look like, that there is nothing good-looking about Him that we should desire him. He told how Jesus would suffer for the whole world, how people on the earth would hate him because of his good works. This Jesus knew all to well about sorrows and grief, yet he came down to die for a lost world, because He had so much love for a people that was in big trouble with God. Our iniquities were so great on the earth, God would have destroyed the whole world if Jesus had not died for our sins. God knew we had gone astray, everybody doing whatever made them feel good, the love of many wax cold, we are big liars, so God needed someone that could bear our iniquities. Jesus humbled himself and took on flesh, so that He could take on our sins in our place. He was oppressed and afflicted by sinful men of this world because they believed not that He was the son of God. He was beaten, slapped, seventy-two thorns they set upon his head, they imbedded the thorns in his skin, blood was all over his body, then they made him carry a big log upon his shoulder called a cross. They put nails in his hands and feet; hung Him on the cross, then a Roman soldier speared him in his side and blood and water ran out. Now this Jesus did all this for you and I. No President, Governor, Senator, or Congressman can love us like God does. This was his only Son that gave his life for a lost world. This is why in 1976 I decided I no longer wanted to do the things of the devil anymore. That was thirty years ago, and I am still going strong in believing in this God. *"He was taken from prison and from judgment: and who shall declare his generation? For he was cut off out of the land of the living: for the transgression of my people was he stricken. He made his grave with the wicked, and with the rich in his death: because he had done no violence, neither was any deceit in his mouth."* (Isaiah 53:8-9). Isaiah prophesied that Jesus would give his life for a lost generation, and that he would share the grave with sinners and the rich. Now understand this was a good and just man which had done no sin, but because of our transgressions, He was stricken by the wicked. We are some of the most deceitful people on the face of this earth, and we love violence and the devil loves violence, but Jesus loves peace and forgiveness. He never talked badly about anyone he came in contact with. Jesus is all about goodness, loving people no matter who they are, no matter what color their skin is, they are people to him. Jesus doesn't care if you are rich or poor, fat or thin, but what he would love to see is that people all over this world would come to repentance before it is too late. The devil would love to have us all in hell with him. *"For unto us a child is born, unto us a son is given: and the government shall be upon his shoulder: and his name shall be called wonderful, counselor, The mighty God, The ever-lasting Father, The prince of Peace."* (Isaiah 9:6).

When Jesus came down here on earth to redeem man back to God, that was a great moment for the world, but we did not know how to accept Him, so we rejected Him. We as a people have been rejecting him ever since, but this is the works of the devil to have you believe God is not real. But I want you to know, not only is He real, He can do all things just because he is God. He took the world upon his shoulders for us because he knew we were a people that was lost without Him in our lives. It is sad that we would rather put our hope in man, than God. You do not have to live in this world with no hope, with no joy, no peace, this Jesus can bring wonderful things into your life. Where there is sorrow, unhappiness, confusion in your life, He is called wonderful, He is called counselor, with him you don't have to pay high fees for his help. Jesus loves us so much He will help you in the time of need and He won't charge you a dime. He is called the mighty God, the everlasting Father, he is Alpha and Omega, the first and last. This is the man we all should want to serve. He is fair, just, and above all He loves us all unconditionally. *"Joseph thou son of David, fear not to take unto thee Mary thy wife: for that which is conceived in her is of the Holy Ghost. And she shalll bring forth a son, and thou shalt call his name Jesus. For he shall save his people from their sins."* (Matthew 1:20-21).

The Jews always knew that the Messiah was coming, but in their minds they thought He was coming looking fine, and having riches, but He was born of a poor woman, and Joseph was really not his earthly father for He was conceived in her womb of the Holy Ghost. The Jews were angry when Jesus called himself the Son of God when He did not have royalty status. This is what the Jews thought to themselves, and many of them would not receive Him. Things were not supposed to happen the way they did, and we, as a people today, have the same problems, wanting to do things our way and not God's way. Many people of today will not accept Him as Lord and Savior of the world. People of today will not serve Him the way the Bible states. Many want to do it their own way. Since you want to do it your way, this is why you have problems in your church, you don't know who to believe anymore because people are big liars. You can't trust your politicians, they are only looking out for themselves, and they are huge liars. God has allowed all these things to come upon the world because we have not truly believed on Him. We live in a world where wrong has become right, and right has become wrong. Everything in this day and time should be about Jesus, for He is the only one that can help us through these troubling times. God is not dead, Jesus has already come down here and taught us about the Father, and one thing He has let me know, God is alive forevermore. We may have our own concept about the things Jesus has said about his Father, because of all the evil things that have happened on this earth.

Many church people have turned wicked because they have lost hope, and no longer want to wait on the Lord. God warned us all these things that are happening must come to pass in these last days, but God is still in control, and man is not, we will not make it without Jesus Christ, the righteous one. The devil understands and knows his time is almost up! The devil hates God and anybody that serves God. So the devil works in whoever lets him. He does not have respect of person, he doesn't care if you are Black, White, Asian, rich, poor, a church goer or a non-church goer, it does not matter to him. I think many people in this world do not understand that Jesus controls this world. The way people have become so sin sick, one would think the devil was in control and had all the power, not so! The things that are happening today, Jesus has already told us they were going to happen. These are some of the things Jesus spoke to his disciples that would come to pass. *"And as he sat upon the Mount of Olives, the disciples came unto him privately, saying, tell us when shall these things be? And what shall be the sign of their coming, and of the end of the world? Take heed that no man deceive you. For many shall come in my name, saying, I am Christ; and shall deceive many. And ye shall hear of wars and rumors of wars. See that ye not be troubled; for all these things must come to pass, but the end is not yet. For nation shall rise against nation, and kingdom against kingdom; and there shall be famines, and pestilences, and earthquakes in divers places. All these are the beginning of sorrows."* (Matthew 24:3-7). All through the books of Matthew, Luke, Mark, and other books of the Bible, one can learn many things about the almighty God, and his Son, Jesus Christ.

There are many people who have a form of Godliness but deny the power thereof. Jesus is great and noble, He laid down His life that sinners may live. He has that much love for sinners. He is a peacemaker and not a peace breaker, as many of us are today. Jesus has so much to offer this world, He is a healer of all manner of diseases, He can cast out devils, we just will not give him a chance. In this walk with the Lord, we must let him be the head of our lives. He is the one that knows what is good for mankind. All races have turned their faces from God to go after the things of this world, which will do your soul no good in the end. Jesus gave up his kingdom to come down here to show man how to get back to God. You know that is so sad, men and women across this world do not want what is right from God, they just want to do there own thing. I remember when I could not stop doing drugs, drinking, smoking, and all the other sinful things that was in my life. Sin had overtaken my life, I did not go for professional help from man, but I remembered all the teachings I got from home. So I called on Jesus to help me overcome my sins. I did not want to serve the devil anymore. I called on Jesus, he heard my prayer, he did not care how rich, how poor, I was, he did not care about the color of my skin, he just came into my life, and my whole way of thinking changed for the better. Once He opened my eyes and I looked back over my sinful life, it shamed me out, the things I used to do. I never want to go back to that lifestyle, I found out Jesus has so much more to offer mankind, the devil just makes people believe he cares for them, and that he can do all things. The devil can't do anymore than we allow him to do to us, we give him power over us. All power comes from God, and God alone. We, as a people need to really know who Jesus Christ is, and know how much he loves us. *"Therefore, being justified by faith, we have peace with God through our Lord Jesus Christ."* (Romans 5:1). *"For when we were yet without strength, in due time Christ died for the ungodly. But God commendeth his love toward us, in that, while we were yet sinners, Christ died for us. Much more then, being now justified by his blood, we shall be saved from wrath through him."* (Romans 5:6-10).

You do not have the strength, nor the know-how to fight off the devil, but Jesus teaches you how to overcome the devil and his works. Jesus through His love, and being justified by faith and the blood of Jesus, I was able to overcome all the wrong that I had done in my lifetime. Christ's death and resurrection releases us to a new life. If you don't have Christ in your life, you are yet dead in your sin. *"Therefore we are buried with him by baptism into death: that like as Christ was raised up from the dead by the glory of the father, even so we also should walk in newness of life."* (Romans 6:4). *"Since then, you have been raised with Christ, set your hearts on things above, where Christ is seated at the right hand of God. Set your affection on things above, not on earthly things."* (Colossians 3:1-2).

One thing that is so sad, and a sickness, is that people would rather honor and cherish a flag, than to depend on God. The flag is just a piece of cloth made by man. The American flag cannot save you, it cannot love you, it did not die for you, Jesus did it all. There are people with flags hanging in their cars proud of a piece of cloth. The American flag gets more respect than God. You can go to jail if you misrepresent the American flag, but children cannot even pray in schools around this country. God is the one who has control over all life in this world. We now live in a confused sick generation of people, and they have no desire to come out of their sins. This is why I use the word sick. The mind is sick when you live in sin. God sees all things we do, nothing is hid from him. God has so much love for us that He keeps on giving us chances to get it right with Him, because He knows he is the only answer to all the world's problems. It is bad when you fall into the hands of a living god, no one, and I mean no one, can help you. Everything in the world belongs to God, and God alone, because God is in control of everything. This is why I want to do God's will because He loves me unconditionally. He has all power, and He does not answer to anyone but himself. Now is the time for all men and women to turn their lives over to God; now is the time for all men and women to turn there minds toward God, and to seek him while He can be found. The world has put God on the back-burner at this point in time. God is very angry with his people because we are nothing but devils. People are doing everything the devil tells them, and then we want to go to church pretending we really know God, and all the time we really do not know Him. People on this earth live a big lie, the God I serve is calling for a righteous, humble people to serve Him.

God sent his son, Jesus, to die for a sinful world, and if He had not died for the world's sins, we would have no hope. I am so glad

Jesus paid the high price for us with his life. People of today have made so many idols their god just to keep from serving the true and living God. Preachers have developed their own agenda, and members are putting all their trust in the preachers, and not God! It has angered God that we have fell so deep into sin, and have begun to serve other gods. Many people are going to have trouble in that great judgment day, then people will find out in that day who Jesus really is, and that they didn't have the right mind in them to go back with this true and living God. All you people out there that think Jesus is not real, or think He is still dead, I want you to know He is still alive forevermore. Some might say, how do you know? Because when I was a sinner, He came into my life and saved my soul from hell. The wrong I used to do, I have no desire to do anymore. Jesus can change your life for the better, it doesn't matter what problems you have, how big or small, it may be a very hard problem for you, but for God no problem is too hard. God just wants people to learn and depend on Him, because He knows what is good for us. We think we know what is good for us, but we as people make multiple mistakes in our lifetime. Some we can recover, some we cannot, but my God makes no mistakes, Jesus wants to bear our burdens, and then He fixes things for us. The problem is we as people do not have a mind to trust in the Lord for all our needs. Trusting in the Lord means we will give God all of us, totally sell out to Him. I want sinners to know the only way you can overcome your sorrows, is by accepting Jesus as the bread that can feed your soul.

"In the beginning was the word, and the word was with God, and the word was God." (John 1:1-11). *"Verily, I say unto you, hereafter ye*

shall see heaven open, and the angels of God ascending and descending upon the son of man." (John 2:52).

To see heaven open and angels all around, this will be good to know that I am a part of this great man who has all power. The angels in heaven respect this great man because they know He is the beginning and end. Now God knows we have not seen Him like his angels have, but if you make your minds up right now that Jesus is the son of God, and ask Him to save you from your sins, He will become your Lord and Saviour right now. *"And as Moses lifted up the serpent in the wilderness, even so must the son of man be lifted up:"* (John 3:14,21).

Jesus chose twelve men to lift his name up in the earth, to tell a lost world to repent of there sins, or in hell they will lift their eyes. Jesus did not stop at just these twelve men, but he has been calling men in to preach His gospel and to lift His name up. I, Dell Watson, also was called by Jesus to lift His name up before this corrupt generation. I did not go to any school, nor do I let any man tell me what to say about Jesus. Jesus himself has ordained me to preach His gospel to a lost people. I am so glad that Jesus has so much love for me that once I told Him I wanted to be saved, He forgave me of all my sins, not a few, but all my wrong. This is why I want the world to know Jesus lives, because He now lives in my soul. I want the world to know it is all about Jesus not man, I put no trust in man for he was born a sinner, and lying is all he knows, unless God saves him, or her, from their sins. Why would you want to lift man's name up, he has been wicked from the foundation of the world. *"He that believeth on the son hath everlasting life: and he that believeth not the son shall not see life; but the wrath of God abideth on him."* (John 3:36).

My goal is to do the will of God, because when I should have been dead, he left me here to help others come to Him before it is too late. Jesus is the best friend anyone would ever need, He is a friend that sticks closer than a brother. Your brother can turn his back on you. We live in a time now, moms and dads may turn their backs on you, but Jesus will never forsake you or leave you. He has just that much love and compassion for a lost and sin sick world. This world is sick minded, church folks are doing what a lot of sinners are doing. I talk with many non-church goers, and what they say now is, "Why should I go to church when church goers are doing the same things I am?" Except we turn to Jesus, we have no hope in this world, or the world to come. It seems to me, we just don't believe Jesus is the holy and righteous one. We serve the devil on each and every hand, proclaiming to love God!. First of all, Jesus, is the Son of God; second, you cannot love God and do the will of Satan. Jesus is the great one who can do all great and mighty things. He is that living water that came down from heaven. *"Whosoever drinketh of this water shall thirst again: But whosoever drinketh of the water that I shall give him shall never thirst; but the water that I shall give him shall be in him a well of water springing up into everlasting life."* (John 4:13-14).

Jesus is everlasting life, and He is that mind regulator when you think your mind is about gone. Jesus can speak to your mind and give it peace, He is that healer that can speak the word, and you will be healed. He does not have to do an EKG to check your heart, he is the heart fixer. What I love about this Jesus is, that He can make a way out of no way. There have been times I did not know how I was going to make it, but Jesus always brought me out of my bad situations smelling like a rose. Jesus has called us to repentance, you know you need to change your life, you know you need to change your way of living, and how you think. I am not impressed by the things on this earth, and neither should you. When God called me out of sin, He called me with a holy call, and I believed on Him when he spoke to me. He is calling you to live a saved life. I know without a doubt, this Jesus rose from the dead with all power in Heaven and earth. *"I am that bread of life, Your fathers did eat manna in the wilderness, and are dead. This is the bread which cometh down from heaven, that a man may eat thereof, and not die. I am the living bread which came down from heaven: if any man eat of this bread that I will give is my flesh, which I will give for the life of the world."* (John 6:48-51).

The prophets in the old testament when they were in the wilderness, God rained down bread for them to eat, and they still died, but Jesus is saying, "I am the bread of life if you take my flesh you will be saved and never die."

In today's society people in church just go to church because it is the number one tradition, they are not really seeking Jesus. They are listening to the preacher, never reading the Bible for themselves. They do not know if the preacher is quoting the scripture right or wrong. This is why so many people today are confused about the Word of God, but let me tell you the truth, if you are going to please God and you want to go to Heaven you must study the word of God for yourself. He requires this of us. *"Search the scriptures; for in them ye think ye have eternal life: and they are they which testify of me."* (John

5:39). When you search the scriptures correctly, you may find out you are not where you need to be with God. Now His disciples are eye-witnesses to everything He did on the earth. Jesus made them preachers so that they can testify to everything they saw Him do. Jesus loved his father so much, and He also loved me and you so much, that He laid down his precious life for no-good sinners like us. *"Labour not for the meat which perisheth, but for that meat which endureth unto everlasting life, which the son of man shall give unto you: for him hath God the father sealed. This the work of God, that ye believe on him whom he hath sent."* (John 6:27-29). God is telling us not to labour and work hard for the worldly things, because they are not for ever, but He is that everlasting bread we all need for our souls. Serve God, and do His works by living holy, no matter what people may say about you. We must remember when we serve God, the devil is mad, but he is not mad at you, but he is angry with God. *"But ye denied the Holy One and the Just, and desired a murderer to be granted unto you: And killed the Prince* of life, whom God hath raised from the dead, whereof we are witnesses."* (Acts 3:14-15). Jesus' disciples are telling the rulers and people of Israel how they denied Jesus before Pilate, and told Pilate, who was the Governor, we rather a murderer go free than to let Jesus live. The sinners did not accept Him as God, so they did not believe in Him and they killed Him. But, on the third day as He stated, He rose from the dead, and this is what his disciples were talking about. They were eye-witnesses that He did rise from the dead.

People of today are just like the people of old. You do not, and will not, believe on the only begotten Son. He is the prince of life, and any man or woman who is not a child of God, must be a child of the devil. Once again, I want the world to know Jesus is alive forever. *"And it shall come to pass that whosoever shall call on the name of the Lord shall be saved."* (Acts 2:21). God loves everyone, I do not care what other people tell you, God will forgive all your sins and cast them into the sea of forgetfulness, never to be remembered by Him. *"The God of our fathers raised up Jesus, whom ye slew and hanged on a tree. Him hath God exalted with his right hand to be a prince and a saviour, for to give repentance to Israel, and forgiveness of sins. And we are his witnesses of these things; and so is also the Holy Ghost, whom God hath given to them that obey him."* (Acts 5:29-32). Once more the disciples are telling the people about this great Jesus, and how they witnessed everything He did before He died, and the things He did when he rose from the dead. *"And it shall come to pass, that every soul, which will not hear that prophet, shall be destroyed from among the people."* (Acts 3:23).

Every person that will not hear a preacher, and believe that Jesus is the Son of God, God will destroy them with the second death, and hell fire.

CHAPTER SEVEN

"Oh Foolish America, Who has Bewitched You?"

Looking back on the 2000 Presidential election, I saw America go back fifty years when blacks could not vote in Florida. What happened in Florida was a shock to many people, blacks were turned away from the polls. We have become a country that would rather live a lie, than to deal with the truth. As I have said many times before, wrong has become right, and right has become wrong in our society. Deep down inside many Americans' hearts, they know the 2000 Presidential election was stolen from Al Gore. However, no one had the guts to stay the course and find out what really happened in Florida. It is things like this that have created American hypocrisy. The American people will tell you they believe in God, but many of them are not living according to the ways of God. So the question is, who has caused the American people to become so weakened?

Life seemed so simple when I was about five or six years old. I was young, but it was possible to see that a great number of people had God in their lives. Adults loved to go to church and take their children; they were serious about God. I can remember when people could sleep with their doors unlocked, one could sleep all night outdoors and not have to worry about safety issues.

Just fifty years ago apples smelled like apples, oranges smelled like oranges, peanuts tasted like peanuts, but our fruits today are filled with many different chemicals, so they can grow faster. The chemicals used to help fruit grow faster take all the natural taste and smell from them. The same with all other foods, they are filled with chemicals. We want everything fast, we drive fast with no respect for anyone else on the road. Road Rage is on the rampage across the entire United States. What is amazing about all these so-called church people or should I say so-called Christians, they are going along with or involved with what sinners are doing. This is why so many sinners say church people can't tell them anything because they see the church committing sinful acts, especially preachers. I am always hearing people say you can't trust preachers. Sinners have heard priests sexually abusing young boys. They have seen preachers fall because of greed, the love of money and women has consumed many of them, but what I want sinners to know, is man will fail you because of his sinful nature. Jesus Christ the righteous will never fail you. He loves the whole human race, the problem is we as people put so much trust in man, and man can't help you in the time of need. Jesus will always be there for His people. If we the people of America are going to make it in these last and evil days, we must love and look to God for all our help. If we would only fall on our knees, or go in our closet and really cry out to God.

Noah preached one-hundred and twenty years, and while he was preaching, he was also building an Ark. Noah told the world during all those years to repent for the kingdom of heaven is at hand. The people did not listen to Noah, they loved their sin nature more. God wiped everyone off the face of the earth with a flood, except for eight people, because of the world's sin. He did this because the people would not change their wicked ways. God would love for everyone to enter Heaven, He wants every man and woman, boy and girl to have the right to the Tree of Life. God does not like the sin that His people have got entangled with. With sin in our life no man can see God in that day, unless he is converted by the blood of Jesus Christ. For there is no sin in God, so when you sin, you sin by the hands of your father the devil, for he is a sinner.

I wish that all people knew how much they really need God. Man can't succeed at anything if it is not in the will of God. We seem to put our trust more in man and not God. We are looking to man and not God. We are looking to man to keep us safe, so another 9/11 won't happen again. I do not care what man has put in place to try and keep America safe from terror, he doesn't have the answers, only my Father has the answers. God is in control of the whole world, and the whole world belongs to him. You know what is so good about this God? He has so much love and compassion for us all. *"O foolish Galatians, who hath bewitched you, that ye should not obey the truth, before whose eyes Jesus Christ hath been evidently set forth, crucified among you?"* (Galatians 3:1).

It seems to me that people do not want to obey the truth anymore, because they are so wrapped up in worldly goods. Your flesh will die, and if you don't die in Christ; in hell you will lift your eyes. Jesus gave his life so we would not end up in hell. Jesus asked the Galatians who has bewitched you, they were in so much sin. He wants to know what causes you to become a weak people. He knew the answer, but He wanted them to come to themselves and think about the wrong they were engaging in. *"Who gave himself for our sins, that he might deliver us from this evil world, according to the will of God and our Father. To whom be glory forever and ever amen."* (Galatians 1:4-5). God sees all the wrong you do and He wanted to remind the church in Galatians, my Son died for your sins that you might be saved from the evil deeds of this present world. Now since Jesus died for our sins, and God the father was in agreement with it, we are to give all glory and honor to the Father. If you think for one minute that this old world loves you, or think it is your friend, you are badly mistaken. Jesus Christ is the way, the truth and the life. The things of this world only last for a little while, but with God life is everlasting. All things are possible for us through Jesus Christ, the son of God. *"Are ye so foolish? Having begun in the spirit, are ye now made perfect by the flesh?"* (Galatians 3:3). It is not about flesh and blood because it will die and return to the dust. It is about your soul. If any man thinks once he or she dies everything is over, they are sadly mistaken. Everyone must understand the flesh means nothing to God, because it is going back to the ground. Your spirit is what must stand before God in that Great Day. *"Be not deceived; God is not mocked: for whatsoever a man soweth, that shall he also reap. For he that soweth to his flesh shall of the flesh reap corruption;*

but he that soweth to the spirit shall of the spirit reap life everlasting." (Galatians 6:7-8).

It pays to be good to all men, for great is your reward with God. If you have sown bad seeds all your life, you will reap bad seeds before you die, this would be the first death. Then, you will be cast into the everlasting fire; to burn forever and ever, this is the second death. We must treat all people with respect and love so that we can have everlasting life with God.

Let me share a few things in the Bible that will keep you out of Heaven. God despises these acts and wishes that we would not commit them. *"This I say then, walk in the spirit and ye shall not fulfill the lust of the flesh. For the flesh lusteth against the spirit and the spirit against the flesh, and these are contrary the one to the other. So that ye cannot do the things that ye would. But if ye be led of the spirit, ye are not under the law. Now the works of the flesh are manifest, which are these; adultery, fornication, uncleanness, lasciviousness, idolatry, witchcraft, hatred, variance, emulations, wrath, strife, seditions, heresies, and envying. Also, murders, drunkenness, revellings, and such like: of the which I tell you before, as I have also told you in time past, that they which do such things shall not inherit the kingdom of God. But the fruit of the spirit is love, joy, peace, longsuffering, gentleness, goodness, faith, meekness, temperance against such there is no law. And they that are Christ's have crucified the flesh with the affections and lusts. If we live in the spirit, let us also walk in the spirit."* (Galatians 5:16-25).

America is in great trouble with the almighty God, and yet we are still acting foolish. Devil worshippers are doing any, and everything they want, except what God has commanded us to do. Murder and death are constantly flashed across the TV screen as I watch the news at night. Terrible things are happening across the United States; it is enough to make you sick. We are cold hearted toward one another, and yet we want to call ourselves saints of God. As I have always said, God is a God of all, He does not care what you look like, or what color you are. He does not care if you are rich or poor, Jew or Gentile, He does not have respect of person. The devil has many of us so deceived he knows that he is not going to Heaven because God kicked him out. The devil's job is to get as many people as he can to go to hell with him. He is mad because you have a chance to obtain salvation. You have a chance to live with God in eternal life, and this is worth more than power, money, or fame.

The Clintons:

Former President Clinton was almost put out of the office because of self-righteous hypocrisy. I am not saying what he did was right, but what self-righteous people did to him was not right either. Children saw and heard things that they should not have heard or seen. It was all in the name of power and money. Those hypocrites that tried to condemn him were not looking for justice because of what he did; it was based upon personal issues. This matter that he experienced should have been between God, his wife, and him. We are people who like mess and anything that will bring another person down. We all have skeletons in our closets. The people in government that tried to bring former President Clinton down had skeletons in their closets. We all have sinned before God and if we tell him to forgive us, He will. There are many who wanted to hang the man due to their own personal feelings. The thing that made me sick out of the whole ordeal, was when they said it would be put on the Internet. Now, I am going to show you what kind of hypocrites we have in America. We have laws to stop children from seeing and reading sexual material on the Internet, however, when it came to former President Clinton's sexual behavior, people in charge wanted it on television, and the Internet. The only thing on their minds was crucify him. The news media we have in America are nothing but crooks; they will sell their lie to the highest bidder. We do not want the truth anymore, but whatever makes us feel good. Let me tell you, America is in trouble and we are a corrupt people. Clinton impressed me during his whole ordeal because, he did not have a mother or father to talk to, but he did talk with church leaders around the country and they gave him spiritual advice. When we are faced with problems in our lives we need to call on God. Clinton did not fold like the devil wanted him to, I call that a man. Knowing you did something wrong, but did not bow down because man wanted you to, that is impressive. The mess making did not stop there with his enemies. Any and every time they had a chance to talk badly about the affair they did. Once again, children's ears were hearing and their eyes were reading books. Internet talked about the affair, yet we talk about protecting children from this kind of thing. All his enemies are no better than him; as a matter of fact Clinton has more class than these self-righteous devils. We all are brothers and sisters, and when we see one another in trouble we are to help, not put down or talk about each other. God wants us to be there for each other, the devil wants us to pull each other down to nothing. He also wants us to hurt each other by any means necessary. This is what Clinton's enemies wanted to do to him. Things did not turn out the way they wanted them to. One thing about President Clinton was that he understood who his enemies were and why they were his enemies. The reason so many of us are weighed down with sin is because we do not understand that the devil is our enemy. Also, we do not understand why he is our enemy, you can't love somebody else until you know God and love him with all your mind, heart, and soul. Anytime a Caucasian man showed interest in helping Black people, he has trouble with his Caucasian race. Bill Clinton had a concern for all people through Jesus Christ. America was his greatest concern. John Kennedy also tried to give Black people a fair shake, Caucasian people did not like that. J. Edgar Hoover was one of the men that truly hated the Kennedy family. People do not have to know you to hate you. The only thing that has to happen is that person let the devil get in them, and the devil will do the rest. The only way to overcome evil is with good, and the only way to have good in you is to truly know Jesus Christ as your personal Savior. The only thing Bill Clinton did wrong was try help all people to be quite honest. Bill did more for Black people than Jesse Jackson has ever done. Jackson just rode the coattail of Reverend King to fame, and ran around the country saying, "I am somebody," and got rich off Black people. Through God Clinton put America back on course for all Americans, not just for the rich or Caucasian people. I will always believe Clinton was set-up by the Republicans with Monica. They knew his weakness was women, we all have weaknesses and we should never ever let other people know what our weaknesses are because they will play on it. This is what happened to President Clinton, the Republicans wanted the White House so bad, so did big companies. I will always believe Monica was paid by the Republicans, and many more Americans believe the same way I do, but don't have the guts to say so. Americans have become wicked and God is not pleased with us, we are doing all the ungodly things here on earth in these last and evil days. I personally thank God for Clinton's work as president, because he looked over all the obstacles that were set in his way and let the Almighty God use him. We do not have too many strong men in this world anymore. They are letting women take over and that was never the order or plan of God. All the men and women that were trying to hang Clinton would not have endured what he did. One thing I know is that all those that tried to bring this man down will pay by the hands of God. They handled the situation wrongly and with hate. I am not saying what he did was right, but who are we to judge another man. The Bible says the measure you judge by will be the same measure in which you will be judged. Again I say America is in big trouble with God, not just one race, but all races of people. God doesn't see race He made people, races come from man and his ignorance. In the beginning God never said black or white, nigger or cracker, first class, middle class, third class, all this started by man and his ignorance. We have been thinking the way man wants us to for generations; now God has had enough of our corruption. Man will not forgive but God will; He has just that much love for us. So all Clinton has to do is ask God to forgive him and really mean it. God will forgive him even if his wife does not.

"But the scripture hath concluded all under sin, that the promise by faith of Jesus Christ might be given to them that believe." (Galatians 3:22). *"For this is my covenant unto them, when I shall take away their sins. As concerning the gospel they are enemies for your sakes, but as*

touching the election, they are beloved for the fathers sakes. For the gifts and calling of God are without repentance." (Romans 11:27-29).

We are to love one another as God has loved us, in spite of all our wrong. No one, and I mean no one, can point fingers at William Jefferson Clinton. I believe the scripture and the scripture says we are all under sin, and the only way to come out of sin is through Jesus Christ. If Jesus is not deep in your heart then you are still under sin, He must be in your mind, heart, and soul. You are to love him with all your strength. If all these things were in you, you would have sorrow in your heart for Mr. Clinton. Sin overtook him just like it does all of us at some point and time in your life. When sin overtakes us we want people to be understanding with us, and forgive us and give us a second chance. Mr. Clinton wanted that second chance.

On the homosexual issue again. *"So God created man in his own image, in the image of God created he him; male and female created he them."* (Genesis 1:27). *"And the Lord God said, it is not good that the man should be alone; I will make him a help meet for him."* (Genesis 2:18). *" And the Lord God caused a deep sleep to fall upon Adam, and he slept: and he took one of his ribs and closed up the flesh instead thereof; and the rib, which the Lord God had taken from man, made he a woman and brought her unto the man. And Adam said this is now bone of my bones, and flesh of my flesh. She shall be called woman, because she was taken out of man. Therefore shall a man leave his father and his mother, and shall cleave unto his wife, and they shall be one flesh."* (Genesis 2:21-25).

Also read Ephesians 5:30-31, Mark 10:6-8. Man was not made for man, and woman was not made for woman. It is sin to have same sex relationships ,and God will deal with it in the judgment. Your so-called Christians rarely voice that it is wrong, and a sin. We all go along to get along, as I have said before, homosexuals can justify it all they want, this is the works of the devil and not God. *"And even as they did not like to retain God in their knowledge, God gave them over to a reprobate mind, to do those things which are not convenient."* (Romans 1:28-32). So since people do not want to obey God and follow his laws, He let the devil have their minds, and this mind is called a reprobated mind. Meaning you will do anything that is not pleasing to God, and follow the devil. Many people in America have corrupted themselves, and they are getting worse each day. People that do have morals are closing their eyes to all the wrong around them. This is why homosexuals are coming out of the closet in great numbers. The next time a homosexual tells you God made them that way, and they can't help themselves, tell them that God did not make them that way, sin did. Sin comes from the devil, you see God already told you from the beginning he made them male and female, and God has never made a mistake. We make mistakes each and every day of our lives, now we are living the big lie, God made me this way! Homosexuality has been around since the beginning of time, that is why God destroyed Sodom and Gomorrah. It was a wicked city. They were doing anything they desired until God brought the city down. The city was full of homosexuals. Being homosexual is bad enough, but when you start dragging little innocent children into living with homosexuals, that is another thing. I think it is very sad when the courts allow homosexuals to adopt little children. Children deserve the opportunity to grow-up in a normal environment. God Almighty did not endorse same sex marriages; we as a people do not stand upon or uphold the laws of God. The laws of God are more important than any laws man has made. Man makes his laws, and we find that he breaks his own laws, and man's laws often are just for certain people. The laws of the world were not made to be fair for the black man, but God's laws are the same for the whole world. Somebody may ask what are the laws of God? The Ten Commandments are God's laws, and His ten commandments have never changed. *"Know ye not that the unrighteous shall not inherit the Kingdom of God? Be not deceived, neither fornicators, nor idolaters, nor abusers of themselves with mankind."* (1Corunthians 6:9). When God say's mankind he means women too, so God will punish people with hell fire that practice homosexuality, it is a sin before God. Homosexuals do not have the right to adopt children according to God's law, and His laws are the only one's that matter. Courts all over the United States are going along with this sickness, any form of sin is a sickness and the only person that can help you is Jesus. However, we as a people do not want to live for Him, Jesus is our only hope in this sin sick world. I do believe there are people who are really hungry for the Word of God, but to have God in your life you must call Him while it is day. *"I tell you, nay; but, except ye repent, ye shall all likewise perish."* (Luke 13:3). *"Remember therefore from whence thou art fallen, and repent, and do the first works, or else I will come unto thee quickly, and I will remove thy candlestick out of his place, except thou repent."* (Revelations 2:5). *"And I gave her space to repent of her fornication, and she repented not."* (Revelations 2:21). Homosexuals have become bold and arrogant because people that believe in what's right have become quiet to the wrong that's displayed. As I have always said, God loves homosexuals and I love them too, but God does not like what they do. We have come to a time in our society that we all need to truly turn back to the living God. It is not about money, power, sex, fame, pretty cars, and education. It is not about men showing their bodies, or women showing their bodies, but it is all about Jesus Christ of Nazareth. So I would say to any homosexual that wants to come out of the sin they are in, you can do it with the help of God. The devil will talk to your mind and tell you that you can't change, but God can do anything if you call upon him and mean it from your heart. *"Resist the devil and he will flee from you."* (James 4:7) When man says no, God says yes. He has so much love for a lost world, but we as a people just do not want to turn our hearts to Him for the good. *"Today if ye will hear his voice harden not your hearts."* (Hebrews 3:7-8). God has touched many people's hearts to change their life from sin. Turn from the things of the world, and He shall forgive you, this precious God is worthy to be praised. I want all homosexuals to understand what you are doing is wrong, but God is just and He will hear you, if you go to him in prayer. *"For we have not an high priest which cannot be touched with the feeling of our infirmities but was in all points tempted like as we are, yet without sin. Let us therefore come boldly unto the throne of grace that we may obtain mercy, and find grace to help in time of need."* (Hebrews 4:15-16). God is as close to you as you want Him, He will show you great mercy if you would come to the throne of his grace, and with God there are no requirements, just come!

Men and Women:

We live in a world now where men do not want to be men anymore, and women want to be the man. We have taken our eyes off God and put them on the world. Many times I have been asking God and thinking to myself, where are the men? People who are weak do not know whom to follow anymore. People are not listening to God at all; they have their own agenda. Confusion is sweeping the world because men and women both have this big thirst for power. One thing that I do understand is that God is all power and His Word will never fail. *"But I would have you know, that the head of every man is Christ; and the head of the woman is the man; and the head of Christ is God,"* (1Corinthians 11:3).

So you see, God's Word will stand all by itself without help from man or woman. It does not matter who likes it or not, man is head of the woman, not to mistreat her, but to provide for her and love her through the will of God. We must go back and do it God's way if we are going back with Him. *"For the man is not of the woman; but the woman of the man. Neither was the man created for the woman; but the woman for the man."* (1Corinthians 11:3-15). *"Let the woman learn in silence with all subjection. But I suffer not a woman to teach, nor to usurp authority over the man, but to be in silence. For Adam was first formed, then Eve. And Adam was not deceived, but the woman being deceived was in the transgression."* (1Timothy 2:11-15). *"A bishop must be blameless, the husband of one wife."* (1Timothy 3:2). I say woman is still being deceived by the devil, it is sad that we have come to a time in our life where we think we have to twist the Word of God... it will not work. This is why so many churches have fallen by the wayside, because eyes are no longer focused on what God desires in our life. The book of Timothy and Corinthians break down the instruction for us the way God wants us to do things. God made us and we are here for His pleasure and purpose. The word usurp means: to seize and hold without legal right or authority; take possession of by force. God does not want the woman to go ahead of the man, but He wants her to pray and ask Him to send some strong men and some strong preachers. When God sees us being real with Him, trusting Him, He will move for us. I know men have become very weak physically and mentally, trust me women, God is just as upset about it as you are. One thing I want you to know, God is still in control of the whole world, He just needs people that will call on His holy name. He does not need a woman to start calling herself a preacher; God did not make a mistake when He chose twelve men to be his Disciples two-thousand years ago. He is that same God today and He never changes. Adam was not deceived, but the woman was, and the serpent knew whom to deceive. Today the devil still knows whom to deceive, just as he did when the woman ate from the tree of life of good and evil, nothing happened. However, when she told Adam to eat like she had done, that is when God came on the scene. He said *"Adam where art thou,"* and at that very moment Adam sinned against God Almighty. Men and women have been messing-up from the beginning, and they are always trying to blame one another for their troubles. God said, *"All have sinned and come short of the glory and honor of God,"* so no one is without sin. Everybody on this earth was born in sin. The only way we can be free from sin is to turn our hearts to Jesus Christ before it is too late. God warns before sending destruction. If the

Bible states a bishop must be blameless and the husband of one wife, then how can the wife be a pastor over the man? A pastor is the head of the church; God said the man is head of the woman and his house. The woman is the wife and the husband is the man. There is nothing confusing about that; God has mapped it out plain. Just like Adam and Eve messed things up from the beginning, man is still messing up things today. I want to say to the people that are trying to live this thing right, do not give up. God sees everything that is happening on this earth, and in due time He will make everything right. You just keep holding on and read your Bible. The Bible lets me know God will have the last word, and the Bible is right and man is a liar from the beginning of time. Many of you are living this big lie, but the Lord is upset with us all. You have men and women totally working to make themselves look good before others, and you have homosexuals trying to prove to heterosexuals they belong. Children are so confused with adults they do not know what is correct anymore. All sin has fallen upon the adults of this world with only the Almighty God to turn to. Amen.

CHAPTER EIGHT

Passion To Be Free

There are two kinds of freedom, everyone in the world is not aware of this, but there is. There is earthly freedom and a spiritual freedom. Being a black man, I know what it feels like not to be free, but I have never been worried about the Caucasian man's freedom. My mind is focused on spiritual freedom. Many people feel that once you die, that is the end. On the contrary, I want you to know that there is life after death. All souls must return unto God to be judged for his or her deeds while they lived on earth. You see, earthly freedom did not come without a price, many black people gave their lives for my generation of blacks to have the freedom we now enjoy. I said thank you God for using those strong black leaders in the nineteen forties, fifties and sixties. They stayed the course because God wanted them to. Many of them died for our freedom, they were treated less than human beings. All this is good, but we all should be looking for that spiritual freedom. Now, Jesus gave His life that all men may have this spiritual freedom. *"Behold, all souls are mine; as the soul of the fathers so also the soul of the son is mine: the soul that sinneth, it shall die."* (Ezekiel 18:4). Behold, means "look!" You see all souls belong to God, and He knows where everyone is. He's just that great and powerful, and He will kill all souls that sin by rejecting His son, Jesus, and those souls will die in hellfire in that great and noble day when Jesus shall appear.

I always wanted to be free from sin, and I always wanted to know more about God. The whole world was condemned to sin because of the disobedience of Adam and Eve. The only way out is through Jesus Christ. Sin does not look at color, wealth, weight, or appearance. Sin does not have respect of persons. I am so glad to know that I am free from worldly things and sin no longer has me bound. In 1977, I asked the Lord to save me from my sins, and He delivered me. *"And ye shall know the truth, and the truth shall make you free. They answered him, we be Abraham's seed, and were never in bondage to any man: how sayest thou, ye shall be made free? Jesus answered them, verily, verily I say unto you whosoever committeth sin is the servant of sin."* (John 8:32-34). The people of Israel felt they were free because they were the seed of Abraham. However, Jesus let them know they were born in sin, and except they turn their hearts and minds to Him, they are still a sinner. God revealed to Israel that they were not free spiritually, and when you commit sin, you are not the servant of God, but the servant of sin. For God cannot sin, I will say it one more time, "God cannot sin," He is the God of righteousness. *"If the son therefore shall make you free, ye shall be free indeed."* (John 8:36). Now, what Jesus is saying here, if He makes you free, you are truly free. You cannot be free unless God becomes the head of your life, and you turn from your sins. You must first admit to yourself, and God, that you are a sinner and in bondage. You want to be free to serve him and him only. I don't care how much money you have, if God is not the head of your life you are bound by your money, which becomes your God. Material things are good in their place, but being high minded will not bring you any closer to God. *"Being then made free from sin, ye became the servants of righteousness. I speak after the manner of men, because of the infirmity of your flesh: for as ye have yielded your members servants to uncleanness and to iniquity unto iniquity; even so now yield your members servants to righteousness, to work holiness. For when ye were the servants of sin, ye were free from righteousness."* (Romans 6:18-20).

Once you make up your mind that you no longer want to be a sinner, and turn your eyes to God, you are no longer the servant of sin, but the servant of the most high God. If your flesh overtakes you, and you love uncleanness and have no problem with sin in your life, then you are the servant of unrighteousness. On the other hand when you yield yourself to God, righteousness and holiness is your lifestyle, and then you become free indeed. You feel like the weight of the world is off your shoulders, you feel like a brand new person. You become a very happy person within your spirit, you feel so free. The best feeling in the world is when you turn your life over to God; you feel like somebody, because you become a child of God. You may not have money, you may not be educated, you may not have a big home, but you are God's child. Now, you may be a drunkard, you may be a prostitute, but if you ask Jesus to save you, if you tell Him you want sin out of your life He will give you peace. God is an understanding God,. I know, because once God helped me get off drugs, alcohol, womanizing, and doing all the ungodly things, I truly felt like the world is no longer on my shoulders anymore. With the Lord's help I can face anything, because the true and living God was on my side, He doesn't care about my past. *"For the law of the spirit of life in Christ Jesus hath made me free from the law of sin and death."* (Roman 8:2).

What people need to understand is God is not concerned about your flesh but your spirit. The flesh goes back to the ground, but the spirit goes into eternity, which is either Heaven or hell. Jesus died for the sins of the world, if you live according to his laws, sin and death will not destroy you in the end. So we are now free to live with God forever, nothing to hold us down anymore because we are in the will of the Almighty God. When you are in the will of God you have the right to the tree of life. So, one may say, "how did Jesus make us free from sin?" If Jesus had not died on the cross we would have no chance to be free from sin. Adam sold us out to sin when he disobeyed God. Adam's actions bound the whole world by sin and death, since Jesus gave his life we can now overcome sin and death and have eternal life through Christ Jesus. *"Stand fast therefore in the liberty wherewith Christ hath made us free, and be not entangled again with the yoke of bondage."* (Romans 5:1). God has made me free from sin; now, I am his servant. God wants me to hold onto him even though trouble will come my way. He does not want me to go back to the old things I use to do. This is why He said do not get entangled again with the yoke of bondage. People all over the world are allowing the devil to have control of their mind and body, but know that once you turn your life over to the living God, the devil has to step back. The devil is angry, and he will do whatever it takes to get you back. Men and women, you need to read your Bible daily, pray daily, so you won't fall back into the trap of the devil. When Jesus died on the cross, our spirit was now under truth and grace. I say, thank God for giving his precious Son to die for a sinner like me. *"For all have sinned, and come short of the glory of God; being justified freely by his grace through the redemption that is in Christ Jesus."* (Romans 3:24).

Anybody that tells you they were not born a sinner, they are telling the biggest lie. God said in His Word we all have sinned, that means all people on the face of the earth. The devil is the father of sin, and until we turn our lives over to God we are the sons and daughters of the devil. The only way you can come out of your sins is to first confess that you are a sinner. When you live for the worldly things, you do not have the right to be the son or daughter of the Almighty God. You must live free from sin in the present world, and come unto the knowledge of who God really is, because He truly cares for you no matter what you have done in the past. He will blot out your sins and forgive you, and this will break the bondage of sin that the devil has kept you down with for so long. *"He that spared not his own son, but delivered him up for us all, how shall he not with him also freely give us all things."* (Romans 8:32). God loves us so much that he let Jesus, his beloved Son, die on the cross for a lost and sin sick world. Only God knew the only way people in the world would have a chance, was that Jesus had to give his life. God knew what had to be done, and He did not spare his only Son's life, because they both love us so much. Now that Jesus has died for us all we have the right to the tree of life through him. We can have all good things God has to offer if we only seek his face. The devil would have the world believe there is no hope for us, and he would have us believe God does not love us. The truth is that the God loves us all the same. I am glad I am free to live a righteous life before God Almighty. He has freed me from all the mean evil things this world has to offer. I can remember when Dr. King was fighting for Civil Rights for minorities, he wanted freedom and justice. When the Civil Rights Bill was passed, that was a glorious day for minorities. When I was drowning in my sins and that old devil had me bound and it looked like there was no hope, I told God I was tired of my sins. I asked him to come into my life and deliver my soul from evil deeds. I needed to be released in my spirit. When God saved me that was a great and glorious day for me. I don't care what you have done in your lifetime, if you want Jesus to be your savior, if you want Jesus to be your best friend, just fall on your knees and tell him to come into your life. I am no longer a servant of the devil, but a servant of God and I am glad about it. When you give your life to Christ, there is an inner joy. God is not going to force anybody to serve him, but if you do come to him He will not cast you out. What I have found out since I have been walking with Christ, is He has high principles, and his morals are higher than the Heavens. The devil's morals are lower than the earth, and there is nothing clean about him. Ask yourself a question, if God has all this goodness, why am I a slave to the devil? *"And he said unto me, it is done. I am Alpha and Omega, the beginning and the end. I will give unto him that is athirst of the fountain of the water of life freely. He that overcometh shall inherit all things; and I will be his God, and he shall be my son."* (Revelations 21:6-7). In this scripture Jesus said, He is Alpha and Omega, the beginning and the end. What He means is there is no one before him or after him. He was here before the world was formed and He will be here when the world is no more, because He is all power by himself. He goes on to say if you are thirsty He will give you a fountain of water freely. You have a soul that needs that living water, and He is that living water which flows from breast to breast, and he does not need any help. When you read this chapter and make up in your mind that you are tired of being a slave to the devil, lift your hands up and tell God I want this fountain of water in my life. If you would just overcome the sin that is in your life you can become the sons and daughters of the Almighty God. There is a song that says, "I am free, praise the Lord I am no longer bound," and that is a good state to be in. We often wonder why things happen to us that are not so good, many people feel the world has dealt them a bad hand, and I use to think that when I was younger. I felt this way because one of the biggest things that troubled me all the time as a black man, was being born poor. I grew up curious and wanted to know why Caucasian people enslaved black people? I would ask God these questions all the time. He never gave me an answer, so I stayed upset all the time. It looks like everything a black person wants he has to ask a Caucasian man for. Freedom is a great thing to have, but what I found as I grew older was that spiritual freedom is a lot more important than earthly freedom. *"And the spirit and the bride say come. And let him that heareth, say, come. And let him that is a thirsty come: And whosoever will, let him take the water of life freely."* (Revelations 22:17). God is saying to all people all over the world, come before it is too late. He wishes that all people would turn and listen to the Word of God. He is also saying if you thirst, come now, He is not talking about the natural. If your spirit is talking to you and telling you it wants a change, listen to the spirit and come to the fountain; that fountain being Jesus Christ. You can have this spiritual water freely it does not cost you anything. If you drink this water you will never thirst again. God is not one that has to do things over and over like man. Once God has done something, it is well done. It is people that constantly mess things up for themselves. When you walk with God there is calmness in your life. You do not look or worry about the things of this world. The devil is on the move and he does not want you to be joyful in the Lord, and he does not want you to have peace of mind. Satan loves for us to be a slave to sin. Jesus is the answer to all your troubles. I have come to love Jesus Christ, because He has allowed me to have this living water through him freely. Jesus is the true vine and if we would let him be our source of energy, He will feed your mind, your heart, and your soul with good fruit. This good fruit that will feed your soul is; love, joy, peace, understanding, and patience, all of these things are to be found in Christ Jesus. So let real freedom ring in your heart forever. Amen.